SWISS ARMY KNIFE

CAMPING & OUTDOOR SURVIVAL GUIDE

101 Tips, Tricks & Uses

BRYAN LYNCH

FOX CHAPEL
PUBLISHING

Dedication

To my parents, I can't thank you enough for all that you did. I love and miss you both every day.
To my stunning wife, Nikki, who has never stopped believing in me, listening to me drone on daily
about things I'm sure she has no interest in, and for making me smile and laugh every day. I love you with
everything I have and always will for the rest of our days.

This book was created in collaboration with Victorinox AG, Switzerland, and Victorinox Swiss Army, Inc. US.
©2019 by Bryan Lynch and Fox Chapel Publishing Company, Inc., 903 Square Street, Mount Joy, PA 17552.

Victorinox Swiss Army Knife Camping & Outdoor Survival Guide is an original work, first published in 2019 by Fox Chapel Publishing
Company, Inc.

ISBN 978-1-56523-995-1

The Cataloging-in-Publication Data is on file with the Library of Congress.

To learn more about the other great books from Fox Chapel Publishing, or to find a retailer near you, call toll-free
1-800-457-9112 or visit us at *www.FoxChapelPublishing.com*.

We are always looking for talented authors. To submit an idea, please send a brief inquiry to
acquisitions@foxchapelpublishing.com.

Printed in China
First printing

By their very nature, working with blades, saws, and other pocket knife tools entails a certain level of risk. The author of this book has
tried, to the best of his knowledge and belief, to set out the safest techniques, and to point out all possible dangers to the reader. The
author, the publisher, and the company (Victorinox AG) cannot guarantee that the techniques described will be safe for everyone to
perform. As such, they assume no responsibility for losses or damages, nor any liability for claims that may be raised in direct or indirect
connection with the contents of this book.

Note that for all outdoor activities, the respective regulations relating to the protection of nature, plants, and animals apply, as do the
weapons legislations in force.

Acknowledgments

First I would like to thank my parents: Dad, for giving me my first knife, without which I would not have had the experiences I have had, and Mom, for letting me keep the knife and for always encouraging me in my writing journey! To my editor, Bud Sperry, thank you for bringing this opportunity to me and guiding me through the process of putting a book together. And thank you to everyone at Fox Chapel Publishing whose hand touched this book and helped to push it toward publication. To the Elsener family, thank you for creating a quality, everlasting product that I could write about. To Victorinox, thank you for providing information and resources that helped in the creation of this book. To my friends, Greg, David, and TJ, thank you for teaching me what you have and guiding me in this field. And to my wife, thank you for taking photos, for your artistic input, and for reading this book so much that you probably know it better than I do.

About the Author

Bryan Lynch grew up in the Midwest state of Iowa, where the state slogan is "Fields of Opportunity." He spent most of his life walking those fields as an avid hunter and fisherman. It was there as a young boy that he learned the value of having a quality knife when his dad gave him a Swiss Army Knife. That first knife sparked a lifelong journey, although some might call it an obsession, into the world of knives, the outdoors, and the gear that is used. Now living in Illinois, he uses his experiences and interests to write about emergency preparedness techniques, survival situations, and gear reviews. Check out his survival blog at *https://civilizedsurvival.blog/*.

CONTENTS

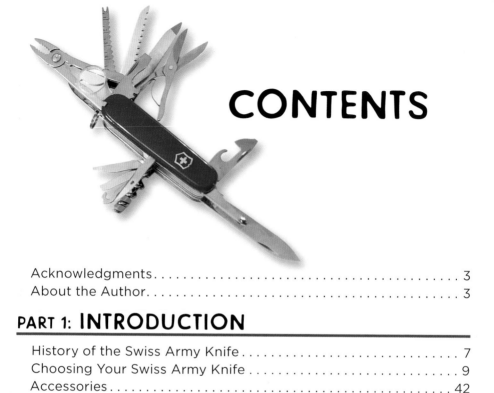

PART 1: INTRODUCTION

PART 2: PREPARATION

6

47

PART 3: USING YOUR KNIFE IN THE WILD

PART 4: URBAN USES

INTRODUCTION

The SwissChamp XAVT model boasts an impressive number of functions—80 in all!

History of the Swiss Army Knife

The story of the Swiss Army Knife began over 130 years ago. In 1884, Karl Elsener established a cutlery shop in Ibach, Switzerland. He developed a remarkable plan to make a compact knife of high-quality steel that also offered a variety of functions. The first model—the Soldier's Knife—was produced in 1891. Sold to the Swiss Army, it contained a blade, can opener, reamer, and screwdriver. It allowed soldiers to service their rifles and open cans of food. The model that most people recognize today is the Officer's Knife, which was patented in 1897. Versions of this knife are still widely popular.

This is the original Swiss Army Knife factory as it stood in 1884.

Karl Elsener (1860–1918).

It wasn't until 1909 that Karl Elsener chose the brand name "Victoria," in memory of his mother, and the emblem of the cross and shield. In 1921, stainless steel (inox) was invented and was a major development for the knife industry. The words *Victoria* and *inox* were then combined to create the new brand name *Victorinox*. Ten years later, in 1931, Carl Elsener II introduced automation in the making of the knives. This helped to ensure that all knives made by Victorinox were produced with consistent high quality.

The popularity of the Swiss Army Knife grew in part because of American soldiers stationed in Europe during World War II. They bought the Swiss Army Knife in large quantities and then took them home with them, where the little red knife quickly became popular with the American public. The knife began its journey out of our world in 1978, when NASA placed an order for the Master Craftsman model to be used by astronauts.

Every Swiss Army Knife is produced in Switzerland at either the Ibach or Delémont factory. Even with today's technology, there is still a surprising amount of human presence in the making of these wonderful knives. Every day, 60,000 Swiss Army Knives are produced and inspected in the Ibach factory. Victorinox has continued to grow in an ever-changing world by also offering cutlery, travel gear, watches, and fragrances. One thing has not changed though: Victorinox is still owned and operated by the Elsener family. And they still make fantastic knives!

Careful inspection ensures the high quality of Swiss Army Knives.

Automated Victorinox factory, 1943.

Choosing Your Swiss Army Knife

The first step in making sure your Swiss Army Knife experience is a great one is to choose the right model. To do this, evaluate your needs. Do you spend more time in urban settings or in the wilderness? Do you like to accomplish DIY projects or just normal everyday tasks? Are you more likely to be gutting a fish or cutting open a box? Determine your interests and needs, and take a look at the vast line of Victorinox models. Each of them offers something different, but all have Victorinox's famous craftsmanship, durability, and versatility.

A WORD OF ADVICE

Local and state regulations may restrict what type of knife may legally be carried outdoors, especially in regard to blade length. Make sure you are not violating any rules.

Midnite Manager

The Midnite Manager is a great example of one of the small models that Victorinox offers. It's what many people picture when they think of a Swiss Army Knife. At 1.1 ounces, the Midnite Manager comes with ten tools. Two of the coolest tools are a pressurized ballpoint pen and an LED light. Holding down the iconic Victorinox logo turns on the surprisingly bright light. A slide button extends the pen point. A different variation comes with a removable 16GB USB drive. This model makes for a great EDC (everyday carry) knife for any urban dweller.

BASIC TOOLS & FUNCTIONS		
1. **LED**	5. **bottle opener**	8. **nail file**
2. **pressurized ballpoint pen**	6. **wire stripper**	9. **screwdriver, 2.5 mm**
3. **key ring**	7. **Phillips screwdriver 0/1, magnetic**	10. **scissors**
4. **small blade**		

Midnite Manager

The Midnite Manager is an ideal EDC knife for the average urban professional who might need the occasional tool in a pinch.

SwissChamp XLT

The SwissChamp XLT is like the standard SwissChamp but with a little bit more emphasis on urban uses. Two of the main differences between the XLT and the standard model are the added pharmaceutical spatula and bit wrench with eight total bits. With the addition of an electrician's blade, the XLT is great for the person with a long "to-do" list.

BASIC TOOLS & FUNCTIONS

1. reamer, punch and sewing awl
2. can opener
3. screwdriver, 3 mm
4. bottle opener
5. screwdriver, 6 mm
6. wire stripper
7. Phillips screwdriver 1/2
8. magnifying glass
9. pliers
10. wire cutter
11. wire-crimping tool
12. screwdriver, 2.5 mm
13. pruning blade
14. electrician's blade
15. wire scraper
16. pharmaceutical spatula
17. multipurpose hook
18. scissors
19. fish scaler
20. ruler (inches)
21. ruler (cm)
22. hook disgorger
23. wood saw
24. chisel, 4 mm
25. nail file
26. metal saw
27. metal file
28. nail cleaner
29. large blade
30. small blade
31. key ring
32. toothpick
33. tweezers
34. pressurized ballpoint pen
35. pin, stainless steel
36. mini screwdriver
37. corkscrew
38. bit, slotted 4
39. bit, Phillips 2
40. bit, Phillips 0 (Pozidrive)
41. bit, Phillips 1 (Pozidrive)
42. bit, Torx 10
43. bit, Torx 15
44. bit case
45. bit wrench
46. female Hex drive, 5 mm for D-SUB connectors
47. female Hex drive, 4 mm for bits
48. bit, Hex 4
49. bit, Torx 8

SwissChamp XLT

The flip-out bit holder securely holds onto the bits so you never have to worry about losing them.

Work Champ

The Work Champ is the SwissChamp's big brother. It's the ultimate portable toolbox. Any hardworking individuals with this robust tool by their side will make their day much easier.

BASIC TOOLS & FUNCTIONS

1. large blade
2. bottle opener
3. screwdriver, 5 mm, lockable
4. wood saw
5. metal saw
6. metal file
7. can opener
8. screwdriver, 3 mm
9. wire stripper
10. reamer, punch
11. Phillips screwdriver 0/1, long
12. scissors
13. Phillips screwdriver 1/2
14. pliers
15. wire cutter
16. wire-crimping tool
17. tweezers
18. toothpick
19. key ring
20. mini screwdriver
21. corkscrew

Work Champ

This portable toolbox offers tools for a variety of situations.

Expedition Kit

Adventures are what make life exciting, but sometimes making sure that you have everything can be a hassle. With this kit, you will have everything. The Expedition Kit combines timeless tools, such as knife, scissors, can/bottle opener, and saw, with modern tech. Placed within the scales of the knife is a digital display, and by pressing the Victorinox logo you can access a thermometer that reads in Fahrenheit and Celsius, a digital watch that reads in 12h and 24h, a countdown, a timer, an altimeter in meters and feet, a barometer, and an alarm. Also included is a sharpening stone and an all-in-one ruler/magnifying glass/thermometer/compass. The only thing more amazing than the craftsmanship of this piece is the fact that all of this fits into a beautiful leather belt pouch.

BASIC TOOLS & FUNCTIONS

1. sharpening stone	15. screwdriver, 6 mm	29. barometer
2. ruler (inches)	16. wire stripper	30. alarm
3. ruler (cm)	17. scissors	31. pressurized ballpoint pen
4. compass	18. nail file	32. pin, stainless steel
5. magnifying glass	19. key ring	33. metal saw
6. thermometer (°C)	20. toothpick	34. metal file
7. thermometer (°F)	21. tweezers	35. nail cleaner
8. spirit level	22. Phillips screwdriver 1/2	36. wood saw
9. large blade	23. digital watch (12h)	37. screwdriver, 2.5 mm
10. small blade	24. digital watch (24h)	38. chisel, 4 mm
11. reamer, punch and sewing awl	25. countdown	39. LED
12. can opener	26. timer	40. mini screwdriver
13. screwdriver, 3 mm	27. altimeter (m)	41. corkscrew
14. bottle opener	28. altimeter (feet)	42. multipurpose hook

Expedition Kit

This kit is perfect for outdoor professionals such as wilderness guides. Or that friend who just loves to have a lot of gadgets.

Fisherman

Your new best friend that will fit nicely in a tackle box slot, the Fisherman is ready to help you cut line, take out hooks, carry fish, and so much more. Don't forget to use the built-in ruler to measure the catch of the day!

BASIC TOOLS & FUNCTIONS

1. large blade
2. small blade
3. can opener
4. screwdriver, 3 mm
5. bottle opener
6. screwdriver, 6 mm
7. wire stripper
8. reamer, punch and sewing awl
9. Phillips screwdriver 1/2
10. scissors
11. fish scaler
12. ruler (inches)
13. ruler (cm)
14. hook disgorger
15. multipurpose hook
16. toothpick
17. tweezers
18. key ring

Fisherman

This useful model offers fishermen an assortment of useful tools.

Evolution S54

The Evolution S54 looks like it can do it all! Have some light-duty maintenance in mind? No problem, it comes with a nut wrench and adjustable pliers. Need to start a fire? No problem, it has a magnifying glass. The built-in ruler and compass are sure to help you get through the woods and to your next secret fishing hole. The safety-conscious trekker will appreciate the locking mechanism on the knife blade of this medium-sized model.

BASIC TOOLS & FUNCTIONS

1. key ring	12. screwdriver, 3 mm	23. wire-crimping tool
2. toothpick	13. reamer, punch and sewing awl	24. nut wrench
3. tweezers	14. wood saw	25. adjustable opening
4. large blade	15. magnifying glass	26. scissors
5. nail file	16. screwdriver, 3.5 mm	27. metal saw
6. nail cleaner	17. compass	28. metal file
7. corkscrew	18. ruler (cm)	29. fish scaler
8. bottle opener	19. ruler (inches)	30. hook disgorger
9. wire stripper	20. sight line	31. Phillips screwdriver 1/2
10. screwdriver, 5 mm	21. pliers	32. universal wrench M3, M4, M5
11. can opener	22. wire cutter	

Evolution S54

I like how a metal frame was used for the magnifying glass on this model.

Spartan

As far as medium models go, you can't get more classic than the Officer's Knife, and the Spartan falls right in line.

BASIC TOOLS & FUNCTIONS

1. large blade
2. small blade
3. can opener
4. screwdriver, 3 mm
5. bottle opener
6. screwdriver, 6 mm
7. wire stripper
8. reamer, punch and sewing awl
9. corkscrew
10. toothpick
11. tweezers
12. key ring

Spartan

With twelve basic tools, the Spartan is an EDC knife for everyone.

Hercules

This model feels as slim as a medium knife but in a robust package. I have always liked the Swiss Army Knife's large straight knife, and using the even larger knife of the Hercules is quite a treat.

BASIC TOOLS & FUNCTIONS

1. large blade
2. can opener
3. screwdriver, 3 mm
4. bottle opener
5. screwdriver, 5 mm, lockable
6. wire stripper
7. reamer, punch
8. Phillips screwdriver 0/1, long
9. scissors
10. toothpick
11. tweezers
12. key ring
13. wood saw
14. corkscrew
15. Phillips screwdriver, 1/2
16. pliers
17. wire cutter
18. wire-crimping tool

Hercules

Just as the name indicates, the Hercules is a large, strong knife ready for some tough jobs!

Choosing Your Swiss Army Knife

The Locksmith

Simplicity meets elegance and functionality with the Locksmith. The one-handed-opening straight blade snaps soundly into the blade-locking mechanism, adding a great degree of safety. I hadn't experienced any of the Swiss Army Knives that were designed to be opened one-handed until I tried out the Locksmith. I have to say that its operation is very smooth.

BASIC TOOLS & FUNCTIONS

1. large blade
2. reamer, punch
3. can opener
4. screwdriver, 3 mm
5. bottle opener
6. screwdriver, 5 mm, lockable
7. wire stripper
8. wood saw
9. metal saw
10. metal file
11. Phillips screwdriver 1/2
12. key ring
13. toothpick
14. tweezers

The Locksmith

In case you are wondering, the "hole" in the large blade is there to allow the blade to be opened with one hand.

The Hunter

The Hunter is the true companion of any outdoorsman. With a wood saw for firewood collecting, a small gutting blade, and a large straight knife for all your cutting needs, what more could you ask for in a tool on a hunting trip?

BASIC TOOLS & FUNCTIONS

1. large blade
2. can opener
3. bottle opener
4. screwdriver, 5 mm
5. wire stripper
6. small gutting blade
7. reamer, punch
8. corkscrew
9. wood saw
10. tweezers
11. toothpick
12. key ring

The Hunter

The design of the gutting blade allows for great control around areas that shouldn't be cut into.

Ranger Grip Boatsman

When you're out on the water, the Ranger Grip Boatsman is the tool you're going to want by your side. With a shackle opener, needle-nosed pliers, and removable bits, this model is ready for anything a day on the boat can throw at you.

BASIC TOOLS & FUNCTIONS

1. key ring	7. screwdriver, 5 mm	13. screwdriver, 3 mm
2. toothpick	8. wire stripper	14. shackle opener
3. tweezers	9. large blade with wavy edge	15. marlin spike
4. bit, slotted 4.5	10. reamer, punch and sewing awl	16. needle-nosed pliers
5. bit, Phillips 3	11. corkscrew	
6. bottle opener	12. can opener	

Ranger Grip Boatsman

The hole in the handle located just under the corkscrew is where the removable bits are inserted when used. The handle of the needle-nosed pliers is extremely comfortable to use.

RescueTool

Whether you are a professional first responder or just making your daily commute, the RescueTool is the model you hope you never have to use, but also hope is always there if you need it. While simple in appearance, it boasts some amazing, lifesaving features: a seat belt cutter, a window breaker, a shatterproof glass disc cutter, and a thicker bottle opener that can be used as a mini crowbar. The disc saw and glass breaker are easily removed if new ones need to be installed.

BASIC TOOLS & FUNCTIONS

1. large blade with wavy edge
2. seat belt cutter
3. reamer, punch
4. disc saw for shatterproof glass

5. bottle opener
6. screwdriver, 5 mm, lockable
7. wire stripper
8. Phillips screwdriver 1/2

9. window breaker
10. key ring
11. toothpick
12. tweezers

RescueTool

The phosphorescent yellow color of the knife and holster will make sure you can find this tool when it counts.

Skipper

The Skipper models have sailing-specific tools, such as marlin spikes and a shackle tool, available to make your day on the water easier.

BASIC TOOLS & FUNCTIONS		
1. large blade with wavy edge	7. can opener	13. wire cutter
2. bottle opener	8. screwdriver, 3 mm	14. wire-crimping tool
3. screwdriver, 5 mm, lockable	9. reamer, punch	15. tweezers
4. wire stripper	10. corkscrew	16. toothpick
5. shackle opener	11. Phillips screwdriver 1/2	17. key ring
6. marlin spike	12. pliers	18. lanyard

Skipper

The tip of the shackle tool can be used to deal with tough knots and other cordage needs a fisherman may have.

Hunter Pro

The Hunter Pro stands out because it is one of the few single-blade knives offered by Victorinox. Interestingly, this knife was designed for hunters in the United States, who expect a lot from their hunting knives. The polyamide handle is incredibly comfortable and allows for a firm grip when handling the robust, lockable blade that is designed to be opened one-handed.

BASIC TOOLS & FUNCTIONS

1. **large blade**

Hunter Pro

The Hunter Pro is perfect for the professional hunting or fishing guide.

Swiss Soldier's Knife 08

This Soldier's Knife is the modern version of the knife that started it all. Simple, tough, and highly functional in the field, the Soldier's Knife is the reason that knives made by Victorinox have been carried by Swiss soldiers for over 100 years. Getting back to basics, the Soldier's Knife demonstrates that just a few tools can get a lot of work done.

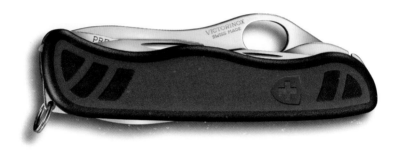

BASIC TOOLS & FUNCTIONS

1. large blade with wavy edge
2. reamer, punch
3. bottle opener
4. screwdriver, 5 mm, lockable
5. wire stripper
6. wood saw
7. Phillips screwdriver 1/2
8. can opener
9. screwdriver, 3 mm
10. key ring

Swiss Soldier's Knife 08

You will not find the tweezers or toothpick on this model, but that doesn't slow the Soldier's Knife down one bit.

Knife Tools and Functions

MODEL	LED	Pressurized Ballpoint Pen	Key Ring	Small Blade	Large Blade	Large Blade with Wavy Edge	Bottle Opener	Can Opener	Corkscrew	Wire Stripper	Wire Cutter	Wire-Crimping Tool	Wire Scraper	Nail File	Nail Cleaner	Toothpick	Tweezers	Mini Screwdriver	Phillips Screwdriver 0/1, Magnetic	Phillips Screwdriver 0/1, Long	Phillips Screwdriver 1/2	Screwdriver, 2.5mm	Screwdriver, 3mm	Screwdriver, 3.5mm	Screwdriver, 5mm	Screwdriver, 5mm, Lockable	Screwdriver, 6mm	Nut Wrench	Universal Wrench M3, M4, M5	Scissors	Reamer	Punch	Sewing Awl	Magnifying Glass	Pliers	Needle-Nosed Pliers	Pruning Blade
Evolution S54			X	X			X	X	X	X	X					X	X						X						X	X	X	X		X			
Expedition Kit		X	X	X	X			X	X	X	X			X		X	X						X						X	X	X	X		X			
Fisherman			X	X	X		X	X	X					X		X	X						X							X	X	X					
Hercules			X	X	X		X	X	X	X	X			X		X	X						X				X				X	X	X				
Hunter Pro			X		X																																
Midnite Manager	X	X	X	X				X	X					X		X	X						X						X	X	X	X		X			
Ranger Grip Boatsman			X	X	X		X	X		X	X												X						X	X	X	X					
RescueTool			X			X							X									X								X	X	X					
Skipper			X	X	X		X	X		X	X												X						X	X	X	X					
Spartan			X	X	X		X	X	X					X		X	X						X								X	X					
SwissChamp XLT	X	X	X	X	X		X	X	X	X	X		X	X		X	X						X				X		X	X	X	X		X			X
Swiss Soldier's Knife 08			X		X					X	X		X										X						X	X	X						
The Hunter			X		X		X	X	X							X	X						X								X	X					
The Locksmith			X		X																										X	X				X	
Work Champ			X	X	X		X	X	X	X	X		X	X		X	X						X				X	X	X	X	X	X		X			

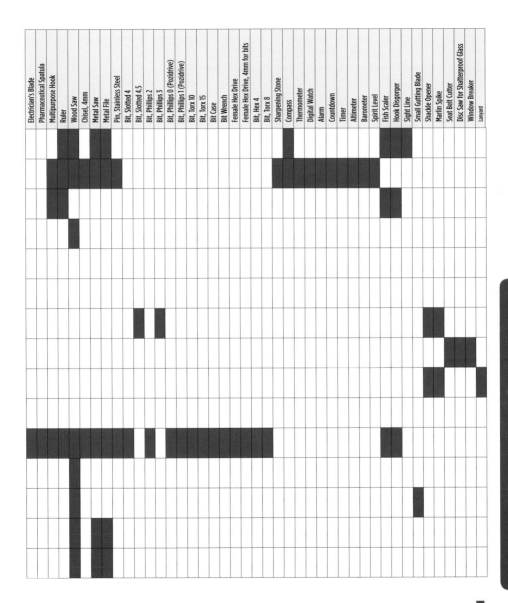

Accessories

All tools need a little love and care from time to time, and the Swiss Army Knife is no different. Using the multi-tool oil (see page 49) will ensure that your Swiss Army Knife continues to function as flawlessly as it did on the day you unboxed it.

The metal chain combines style and function for any Swiss Army Knife owner. The main clip, which is stamped with Victorinox's logo, attaches to your belt. There are two chains that branch off to attach a key and your Swiss Army Knife.

This little bottle doesn't take up much space so it can always fit in your pack.

You won't lose your Swiss Army Knife when it's attached to the chain and clip. Pieces can be removed from the clip and chains for other purposes if needed.

Tired of digging around in your pockets for your Swiss Army Knife? There are different styles of belt pouches available: small, large, leather, or nylon. These pouches help keep your Swiss Army Knife protected while remaining accessible at all times.

Victorinox offers a dual knife sharpener that is very compact. It is roughly the size of a fountain pen.

A bonus of having a leather pouch is that it can be used as a strop for sharpening a knife in the field.

After removing the cap, there is a removable two-sided sharpener. A V-shaped ceramic sharpener is on one end for fine-tuning an edge.

The pocket clip ensures that you know where your sharpener is at all times.

Flipping the sharpener around allows you to use the stone sharpener, which will aid in restoring a very dull edge. I like that the stone sharpener has a groove down the middle for sharpening fishhooks.

Accessories

The smaller, unfixed tools of the Swiss Army Knife, such as the pin, pen, tweezers, and toothpick, can be easy to lose—mainly due to their size, not because they would ever fall out of the frame. Other parts, such as the springs and the key ring, may simply wear out after years of use. If you find yourself in this situation, don't worry, because all these parts can be ordered individually from Victorinox. Of course, the true Swiss Army Knife fan who has several different models will have the replacement parts kit, which is filled with toothpicks, tweezers, pens, key rings, and springs. Everything is well organized inside a plastic container and is kept safe by an exterior slide lock.

The kit comes with an inventory list that specifies the different sizes of the small replacement tools, as well as their location within the box, just like a box of chocolates.

Adding Your Own Accessories

Packed with several tools, the Swiss Army Knife takes the place of several items in your pocket or pack. You won't have to carry around the extra weight of several tools. As handy as the Swiss Army Knife already is, there is still more that can be done with it.

Pictured below is what I would call the most basic survival kit that one can make with the Swiss Army Knife. This is my personal SwissChamp, which I believe to be one of Victorinox's best models. I've added a few items of my own. Making fire is critical in many situations, so I included a ferrocerium rod. Extra key rings help in attaching tools and have a multitude of other purposes. A signaling whistle can alert anyone to my presence. I have also added some small lengths of cordage. Paracord may seem bulky, but when wrapped up it fits comfortably in one's pocket. The tools I included can easily be removed from the key ring, but they make it a nice, inclusive kit.

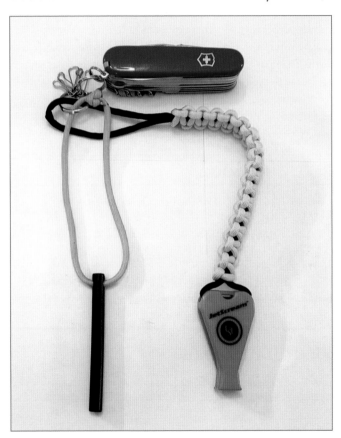

The SwissChamp with a ferrocerium rod, a whistle, paracord lanyards, and extra key rings.

As full as the Swiss Army Knife is, there is still some space that you can use, so why not use it? The corkscrew on the SwissChamp is located so that the space around it can be used to store different materials. A ferrocerium rod, for example, can be cut to size and placed there.

There are many different ways in which you can modify and add to your setup. Take time to figure out what you need from your Swiss Army Knife, then make it your own!

NEW LOOK

Want a new look for your trusty tool? It's as easy as popping off the old scales and pressing on the new ones.

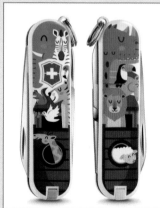

Winning designs from a recent Victorinox Classic Limited Edition Design Contest. What would your personal Swiss Army Knife look like?

PART 2:

PREPARATION

No matter where you take it, there is a Swiss Army Knife for any situation.

Cleaning, Sharpening, and Maintenance Tips

Cleaning the Swiss Army Knife

Over the years, dirt, sand, and other debris will find their way into the crevices and fine parts of the Swiss Army Knife. This will eventually wear on the parts and make it difficult to open the various tools. Since the Swiss Army Knife is made from high-grade stainless steel and other quality components, it will last for generations if properly maintained. Cleaning and oiling regularly will give it a nice appearance and make sure that it functions the way it is supposed to.

When cleaning, first remove all the tools that are not fixed to the frame. These can be cleaned and wiped down separately.

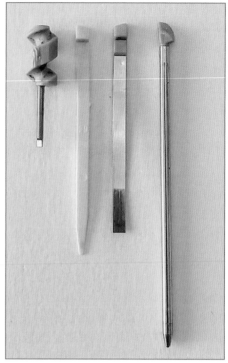

Pictured left to right: miniature screwdriver, toothpick, tweezers, and ballpoint pen.

A WORD OF ADVICE

Do not submerse in water any model that has a flashlight or digital components.

Any small container, such as this plastic tote, will work.

Unless it has electronic components, dip the entire Swiss Army Knife into a container of warm water and swirl it around. While it is under the water, open and close each tool several times to get rid of any dirt and debris that may be in the crevices.

Use a sponge with a soft scouring pad on one side to help scrub away any marks and hard-to-remove dirt. Do not use a harder abrasive such as steel wool or sandpaper. After washing, dry each tool and the frame with a rag or towel. Even though it is made from stainless steel, it needs to be dried thoroughly.

Apply a small amount of the multi-tool oil to any moving parts a tool might have, such as where the two pieces of the scissors and pliers intersect. To lubricate the moving parts, apply a small amount—a single drop—to the hinge points of the tools. Open and close the tools several times to help spread the oil. Wipe down the smaller tools—toothpick, tweezers, etc.—with warm water and put

Cut about half an inch (2.5cm) off the end of a sponge for this step.

them back in the frame. The cleaning process is complete. If you're installing new scales, use a vice grip or pair of pliers to gently squeeze and snap the new scales into place. When compressing the scales, use a piece of cloth or any other type of padding between the vice grip and Swiss Army Knife to prevent damage to the scales.

After applying oil, open and close the tools several times to help spread the oil.

After applying oil to the scissors, stand them upright and open and close them several times to help spread the oil down to the pin.

Cleaning, Sharpening, and Maintenance Tips

Replacing the Springs

In some of the tools, such as the pliers and scissors, there is a spring that can be replaced if it begins to lose tension. Note that the two openings on either side of the frame are actually different in size, with one slightly larger than the other. Look at both sides before taking the spring out and keep track of which side that is. The spring should be pushed out from the side with the

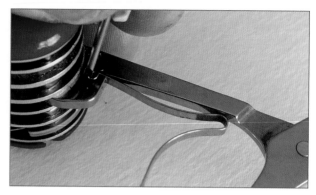

The miniature screwdriver head is small enough to help push out the base of the spring.

One side of the tweezers just fits into the space where the base of the spring sits.

smaller opening, and the new spring should be inserted on the side with the larger opening.

To remove the spring, I use my free hand to push the spring from the top while also pushing at the bottom with either the miniature screwdriver or the tweezers. A small nail or punch that better fits the opening of the spring would be ideal, but if you don't have either of those on hand, these tools can be used instead.

Lay the new spring at a slight angle, and if a pair of pliers are available, use them to gently squeeze the new spring into place. If a punch or a pair of pliers is not available, I like to use the miniature screwdriver. Press in the bottom with the screwdriver while holding onto the rest of the spring with your other hand.

A WORD OF ADVICE

Not all of the springs are equal! When ordering a replacement, check that the spring you are ordering is for the correct Swiss Army Knife model and for the correct tool on that model.

Sharpening the Blade

Every Swiss Army Knife I have ever bought was razor sharp right out of the box and held its sharp edge much longer than other knives I have purchased. However, through use and abuse, even the Swiss Army Knife will eventually need to be sharpened. It is not good enough to have the best tool out there; taking care of it is just as important. A dull knife increases the risk of injury because a lot more force has to be put into the cutting task. And if the knife slips, you will cut yourself with that extra force. It may seem backwards, but I have cut myself more with tools that have dull edges than sharp edges—and it hurts just as much! Keeping the knife sharp is essential.

Pictured left to right: a small dual-sided sharpening stone, a 6" (15cm) three-stone sharpener, a container of water, and a leather strop with a buffing compound. The smaller doubled-sided stone on the far left is an ideal size to place in a go-bag.

TOOLS I USE FOR SHARPENING

- Sharpening stones
- Leather strop
- Buffing compound
- 1,000-grit sandpaper
- Portable sharpeners

SAFETY NOTE

Always wear gloves when cutting and sharpening your knife. After the sharpening process, wash your hands to remove the stone and metal residue from your skin.

SHARPENING STONES

Sharpening stones come in different types and grit levels. Some require lubricants, such as oil or water. Oil tends to be messy and a headache to clean up, so I stick with water or dry stones. Research what the stone needs in order to use it properly, and preserve it for as long as possible. It's important that you do not use too much downward pressure when sharpening an edge. The weight of the knife is all the downward pressure you really need, because you want the stone to do the work.

If the edge is in rough shape, with nicks in the metal, it will need to be ground down. To accomplish this, draw the knife across a metal file as though you are cutting into it. A coarse stone can be used for this step, but I prefer a metal file. With the reamer tool (extended in the photo below), I was able to restore the edge by drawing it across a coarse stone (less than 1,000 grit), then a medium stone (1,000–3,000 grit), several times.

The dullness of the knife will determine which stone to start with. For example, if the knife is brand-new and has only been subjected to light-duty tasks, you will not need to use it on the coarsest stone. Instead, a fine-grit stone (4,000–8,000 grit) should bring the edge back rather quickly. With a little experience, it will become easy to tell which stone to start with.

This reamer tool has nicks all along the blade. This happened because I used the reamer to puncture holes in a metal can for a project. I should have made a straight punch in and out of the metal, but instead I turned the reamer when puncturing.

1. Make sure that the stone is well lubricated. Some stones need to be soaked in water beforehand for a predetermined amount of time, so read up on the kind of stone you are using. The three-sided stone sharpener I initially use came with a small bottle of oil; however, the instructions did say that water could be used. I have used water on it for a long time, and it works just fine. When it comes to the angle of the blade, place the blade flat on the stone, then tilt the spine of the blade slightly upward as if you are trying to slice a thin layer off the top of the stone. Victorinox recommends using a 20° angle when sharpening. I use two fingers on the blade to keep even pressure and help keep the angle constant.

2. Once you have your angle set, work the blade back and forth in a circular motion a few times (or you can use a single-stroke cutting method instead). Flip the blade over and repeat. Avoid overworking one side more than the other, as this will make the edge uneven and therefore not as sharp. Before moving on to the next stone, draw the knife across the stone in the single-stroke cutting method as if you are slicing the top layer of the stone off. Do this several times on each side. Remember to keep adding lubrication throughout the process. You can never have too much. Move from the fine-grit stone (4,000–8,000 grit) to fine-grit sandpaper (1,000 grit). This helps to eliminate any metal burrs and to further smooth the surface of the blade. Use the same motions on the sandpaper as used on the stones.

3. Rub some buffing compound (optional) on the leather strop until a layer of the compound can be seen. (The buffing compound is optional, but it really polishes the blade.) Strop the knife away from the blade's edge side several times. Wipe the blade, and you should now have a clean, polished, and—most importantly—sharp edge.

PORTABLE SHARPENERS

Larger sharpening stones and their accessories might be too bulky to carry with you when you are on the move. Luckily there are some great lightweight sharpeners out there that are much more mobile. Pocket and other portable sharpeners are made for fine-tuning a blade that already has a good edge on it. If the knife has nicks or chips in it, however, portable sharpeners may not be as helpful as a sharpening stone.

Pocket sharpeners are compact and combine the best of both worlds. They typically have two sharpening ports in the shape of a "V." One port has carbide rods for the initial rough sharpening, and the second port has ceramic rods for smoothing out the final sharp edge. These pocket sharpeners are foolproof. Anyone can use them.

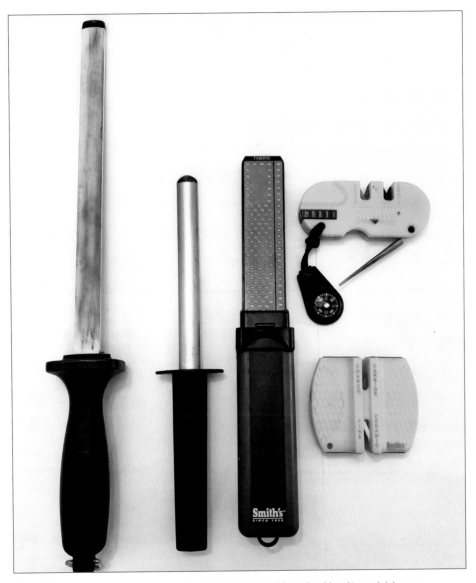

Pictured left to right: ceramic sharpening rod, diamond sharpening rod, diamond sharpening stick, and two pocket sharpeners.

1. Simply insert the knife, tilt the tip of the blade slightly downward, and draw the knife through the "V" as many times as needed. On some of the pocket sharpeners, there is a third sharpening surface that I have found useful: a foldable, cone-shaped rod for sharpening serrated blades and fishing hooks. Remember to always sharpen with the carbide side first and to finish up with the ceramic side.

If you don't have any kind of sharpener on you, you can use a rock to sharpen a dull blade. A rock that is flat and as smooth as possible will work best. The bottom of a ceramic coffee mug can also be used, as the bottoms do not have glaze on them.

Sharpening Other Tools

SCISSORS

Open the handle of the scissors all the way so that you can sharpen one edge at a time with a sharpening stone. There is just the slightest angle on the edge of the scissors so that you can almost hold it upright when sharpening. Move the edge around a few times in a circle and finish with a few straight strokes. Flip the knife over and repeat on the other scissor edge.

This smaller sharpening stone has a fine grit (4,000–8,000 grit) on one side and a coarse grit (less than 1,000 grit) on the other side.

WOOD SAW

When sharpening the wood saw, use the smallest diamond rod (pen sharpener) or smallest file that you can find. Place the sharpener at an angle so that it fits into the groove of the saw blade teeth and slide the sharpener forward several times, taking care not to round off the top of the cutting teeth. After you have moved all the way down on one side, turn the knife around and repeat the process on the opposite side.

CAN OPENER AND CHISEL

Two tools that are often overlooked when it comes to sharpening are the can opener and the chisel, perhaps because they are not used often. I like to use two different sharpening surfaces for these tools.

Because of the small, curved shape of the can opener blade, I like to use a portable sharpener to sharpen it. Just as for sharpening the knife, find the angle of the edge and run the sharpener across the blade in a slicing motion. Clean up the edge with a ceramic stone if one is available.

Due to the shape of the chisel, I like to use a flat sharpening stone to sharpen it. Setting the angle is quite easy, as it has a very deep angle on the tip. Run the stone from the tip

Really take your time when doing this, otherwise you risk rounding off the cutting teeth and ending up with a dull saw blade.

of the chisel backward toward the frame of the Swiss Army Knife until you achieve the desired edge. Flip the chisel over and lay the tip so that it is flat on the stone. Rub this side just a few times to remove any burrs from the flat side.

How to Use Your Swiss Army Knife

To get the most out of your Swiss Army Knife, make sure you know how to safely use it. There are a lot of sharp, moving parts in the Swiss Army Knife. Like any tool, if you do not know how to use it properly it can be dangerous. Many of the tools do not lock into place. However, in the medium and large models, Victorinox has added locking mechanisms to some of the tools, which is a great safety feature.

No Locks, No Problem!

A non-locking blade does not pose a safety issue in and of itself. Not knowing how to use it is the safety issue. Since many of the tools on the Swiss Army Knife do not lock, always fold a tool back into the frame whenever you are done with it. If you choose not to replace the tools, then change the position in which you are holding the knife so that your fingers are only holding onto the scales and are out of harm's way in case one of the tools accidently closes. And never extend more than one tool at a time when using the Swiss Army Knife.

Use the Right Tool for the Job!

Tools should not be used in ways for which they were not intended. There are exceptions to this rule: if you're in a serious situation when there is no other option, or if it is being used for light duty (where the only detrimental effect would be a dull blade, for example). Using the tip or the edge of a knife as a screwdriver or a pry bar will most likely result in severely damaging the blade and should be avoided. A tool that breaks can throw sharp metal pieces in many directions.

> ### A WORD OF ADVICE
>
> When you start cutting, you may have trouble with the saw sliding and not biting into the wood where you want the cut to be. To help start the cut, place the saw teeth where the cut is going to be and pull the saw blade backward several times in single strokes. This should keep the saw from moving side to side during sawing. Sometimes during a cut, the saw will bind or get caught due to the weight of the wood falling in on itself. To prevent this, make an undercut and support the wood when possible.

Cutting Methods

The golden rule of cutting is to cut away from your body. And always have your fingers behind the blade. You should also never cut if you are fatigued.

In many of the projects, I suggest using the wood saw to make a cut. If your Swiss Army Knife lacks a wood saw tool, you can still complete these projects. Although the wood saw makes fast, clean cuts, using the cutting methods below can still be achieved, but they may take longer.

THUMB-PUSHING

Use this method when you need to make precise cuts. Since the cutting strokes are short, you can put more force into the cut while still maintaining control. Place your right thumb on the spine of the blade, your left thumb over your right thumb, and hold the wood in your left hand while pushing the blade with your thumbs (reverse hands if you're left-handed). This is very helpful when cutting notches into wood.

Thumb-pushing is for cutting small areas, detail work, and carving out the inside of notches.

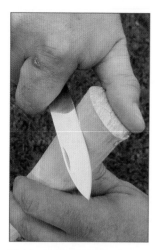

This is the **correct** way to make a draw cut. If the knife slips or cuts through the wood quicker than anticipated, you will not have a bleeding thumb.

This is an **incorrect** way to use the draw-cut because my thumb is at the end of the cut. Ouch!

DRAW-CUTTING

This method goes against the golden rule because the knife is going toward your body. But it is a controlled, slow cut, so the odds of cutting yourself are small.

Use this method when working on the end of a piece of wood or in tight spaces. If you're right-handed, use your right thumb as an anchor point while drawing the knife toward yourself.

The straightaway cut is great for making shavings for fire tinder.

STRAIGHTAWAY CUT

This method is ideal for when you want to remove a large amount of wood in short order and being precise doesn't really matter. Make sure that you keep your wrist as straight as possible and lock it in place. There is a tendency with this method to have the wrist bend sharply while carving away the wood. Bending your wrist is going to hurt after a while and also lead to an uncontrolled cut.

If your wrist is bending too much, it is either because you are cutting too deep or there is a knot in the wood. When there is an offshoot of another branch, do not try to cut it away from the base of that branch. It will usually be too thick to cut straight through it. Instead, cut from the top to the bottom, making small cuts as you go.

BATONING WOOD

Batoning wood is a method of splitting wood by hitting the spine of the blade with another piece of wood. While this can be done with the small and medium models, it works best with the large models. Be extra mindful with blades that don't lock when using this method of splitting wood.

Batoning wood may be done with the small or large blades, but the large blade works best.

A WORD OF ADVICE

If the blade becomes stuck, invert the piece of wood and tap the knife with another piece of wood to back it out of the cut.

USING YOUR KNIFE IN THE WILD

To thrive in an environment like this, make sure you have a Swiss Army Knife on hand.

Intro to Bushcraft and Survival

Bushcraft has become a popular term to describe someone who uses his or her knowledge and skills to live in the wild. While bushcrafters are using survival skills, typically they are not in a *survival* situation. For me, bushcraft centers around the ability to sustain yourself long term comfortably by knowing how to construct shelters, furniture, and tools from the surrounding area. A bushcraft situation is one you are prepared for by having the tools you need to complete the tasks at hand (i.e., axe, chisels, saws, and other carving implements). A survival situation is something you're trying to get out of and are not fully prepared or equipped for. While there are certainly many aspects of bushcraft that apply to a survival situation, they most likely will not be used to the same extent. For example, in a survival situation, not as much time or energy may be spent on building a shelter.

There is also some debate on what a bushcraft knife is versus a survival knife. A knife meant for bushcrafting tends to have a small profile, which makes it better suited for detail work and carving. Generally, a survival knife is thought of as a larger, fixed-blade knife that is capable of digging, cutting, prying, chopping, etc. A survival knife is supposed to do it all because it will most likely be the only tool available.

By my own definition, a Swiss Army Knife is not really a survival knife or a bushcraft knife. Rather, a Swiss Army Knife combines the characteristics of both. However, given the option, if I could have only one tool in a survival situation, I would choose a Swiss Army Knife over a large fixed blade. That is because a Swiss Army Knife can complete more tasks while being safer and saving energy. It will be able to complete finer detail work that is needed in making certain tools and repairing gear.

The Swiss Army Knife is arguably the first multi-tool manufactured and has continued to evolve since its simple yet revolutionary conception. It does not do only one thing extremely well, like a single-purpose tool, and this can be frustrating to some. Instead, multi-tools are light-duty tools designed with many attachments to give the user as many options as possible when a toolbox is

> *"For most of history, man has had to fight nature to survive . . . he is beginning to realize that, in order to survive, he must protect it."*
> **—Jacques-Yves Cousteau**

not available, and thus they may be prone to misuse. Even though they are light-duty tools, they can still complete tough jobs if used properly.

Since I have used a Swiss Army Knife for most of my life, I have never believed the current reality-show lies that we only need one knife and it must be capable of chopping down entire trees or building a small village from logs or defending ourselves from some imaginary force. One of the top reasons I am wary of most of these TV "experts" is because they are using knives that are not really meant for outdoor tasks. When it comes to the detailed work that is involved in camping, hiking, hunting, fishing, and emergency tasks, they just don't work well. A larger fixed blade has its place, but it works best as a complement to a multi-tool such as the Swiss Army Knife. Together, they create a powerhouse of versatility.

Some of you may read my blog, *https://civilizedsurvival.blog/,* created to counter the doom-and-gloom culture. I enjoy steering others to good and appropriate tools and techniques through my website, tool reviews, and now this book. My goal was to put a lighter tone to teaching prepping, "old school" skills, DIY projects, natural skills, hunting tips, fishing tips, and emergency preparedness. I don't want to continue the scare tactics employed by others. Becoming self-reliant should be achieved from the desire to learn and to take care of those you love, not from fear.

In My Experience

Around the age of five or six I received my first pocketknife from my dad. It was a used Swiss Army Knife, but I didn't care that it wasn't new. I didn't use it for several days; I wanted to keep it as it was, perfect. Because my dad had given me one of his tools and trusted me with it, I was proud. Having my own tool, it felt like my first rite of passage. In my young mind, I thought I was finally a man!

The knife became an extension of my body, and I never went anywhere without it. I used it to sharpen sticks, carved letters into pieces of bark, dissected plants, and more. I even tried my hand (unsuccessfully) at whittling. One of my favorite activities was learning how to start fires with the magnifying glass. To my mom's dismay, many scorch marks found their way onto my shoes and pant legs. After all, I had to test the limits of the greatest tool I had ever owned!

I'm glad to have been among what was surely the last generation for whom it was widely acceptable for a kid to carry a knife. Without a cell phone or a computer (and with video games still being a bit of a luxury), that knife encouraged me to be outdoors and gave me a sense of responsibility at a young age. That first knife instilled in me a lifelong passion (though some might call it an obsession) to always have a good knife on hand. Now, as a dad myself, I have had the pleasure of watching my kids use a Swiss Army Knife as I did when I was a boy.

Keeping Your Mind Busy and Your Morale Up

You could say that every day is a kind of survival situation: busy schedules, meeting critical deadlines, caring for loved ones, juggling home and work life. We can plan to some degree on how to cope with this daily stress. More intense survival or emergency situations away from home can take us by surprise. To prepare for the unexpected in the wild, do what you can now to plan for a happy ending.

When a very stressful situation or emergency arises, you can easily become overwhelmed: physically, mentally, and emotionally. I am clumsy on a good day, so during an emergency I am probably going to be tripping over myself. Mistakes are easily made when our body and mind are fatigued. It is extremely important to remember to rest and not overwork yourself when you're facing an emergency situation. On the flip side, being stagnant can be just as dangerous. A friend once told me, "Waiting can be a disease." When I am slowing down more than I should, I try to remind myself of these things.

During an emergency, our gadgets may not work, and the batteries certainly won't last forever. Here are a few things that you can do to stay productive but also relaxed during a stressful situation in the wild.

Write It Down

A writing utensil may not be on most people's outdoor survival plan radar, but having one can give you a significant advantage. And paper can have a ton of different uses besides just writing on it. Plus, the batteries in your gadgets are not going to last indefinitely, so having something else to do can cure boredom. The SwissChamp comes with a ballpoint pen that can help you clear your mind by writing or even just doodling.

Besides curing boredom, the most important aspect of having a writing utensil is that it will allow you to document your journey. There are many important things that we may overlook or forget about if we don't record them—where you have been, for instance. Having eyes on the ground will give you more information than a map will. So recording landmarks or helpful information, such as an old bridge or cabin or game trail, will help if you need to backtrack.

When we are thrust into situations that take us out of our daily routine, it is easy to become overwhelmed. It's important to set

> *"The earth has music for those who listen."*
> —**George Santayana**

daily goals in order to keep motivated and to keep the end result in sight. Making lists is a helpful way to slow your mind down, leave yourself reminders, and organize priorities. I love making lists and crossing out the items that I have completed. It's a morale boost to see that I've accomplished something, and it encourages me to stay productive. The feeling of satisfaction is worth a lot in a stressful situation.

What plans or techniques worked and what didn't work when you faced trouble in the wild? Write it down. Experience is the best teacher. Usually if I do something once, I remember how to do it. But that is not always the case as I get older. Being able to look back in my journal and see how I started a fire the day before is a good resource to have.

Using the pen on the Signature Lite model to take notes in my field journal—and I may be doodling a bit as well.

Speaking of resources, keeping track of resources and their location is incredibly valuable. No matter what kind of situation you find yourself in, it is important to note resources when you come upon them. You may find an area that has a good water supply or abundant wildlife signs, but it may not be a good place to set up camp. Knowing how to get back to that area, and where resources are located, can save you a lot of time. Again, if you have to backtrack, knowing where resources are will help in planning your route. All this information can be helpful reminders down the road when your mind is preoccupied with more pressing concerns.

Whittling

Whittling is one of those classic activities that I think most outdoorsmen try at some point. It is an activity that brings to mind an old-timer crafting a smoking pipe or some type of bird. To be honest, I don't think it matters if you are good at it (I'm not!). What matters is the journey, the process. If it is relaxing and you enjoy it, then that is enough. When you need a few calm minutes during an outdoor trip, whittling can be the perfect way to breathe deep and consider your next steps.

I combined art with semi-functionality when I whittled a very impromptu fork. I also made a small spoon for stirring my morning coffee. In the photo you may notice the handy paracord loops I added for easy hanging. The holes were made with the reamer tool. Keep your eyes peeled for the fork to make an appearance in another project.

I have had better luck with the smaller to medium Swiss Army Knife models, such as the Tinker, when I have whittled for fun. For a more in-depth look at whittling and some great projects, I suggest *Victorinox Swiss Army Knife Whittling Book* by Chris Lubkemann.

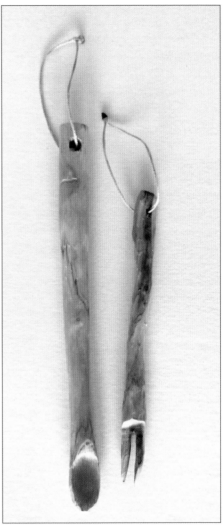

I used the small blade and chisel on my SwissChamp to complete these rough-looking utensils.

Tips for the Outdoors

Breaking Wood

The knife and wood saw are great tools for cutting lengths of wood, but there are times where you just need to break a branch into a smaller piece for firewood and the ends don't matter. I remember one night around the campfire when my dad started laughing at me for having difficulty breaking a piece of wood. When I was younger, I either stood on one end while bending it or I would use my knee to press into the center of the branch while pulling the ends. He told me that I was working harder not smarter. He pointed out a nearby tree and showed me that by putting the branch in between the crooks of the branches you could use the tree as leverage to break the piece of wood. This saved my knees from years of pain.

Quick Measurements in the Field

Not all Swiss Army Knives come with a ruler tool. Even if they do, it can take quite a while to measure something a few inches at a time. Having a way to measure larger distances quickly can be a big help. One trick I learned years ago from my dad was how to use my body to measure materials in the field. Aside from the commonly used estimation

of 12 inches (30cm) for your foot, there are three different reference points that I use quite often. The distance from my fingertips to my armpit is just over 2 feet (61cm). With my left arm outstretched, the distance between my right hip and the fingertips of my left hand is 4 feet (122cm). When both of my arms are stretched out to the side, the distance from the fingertips of one hand to the other is roughly 5 feet (152cm). Obviously everybody is different, so premeasure your own limbs.

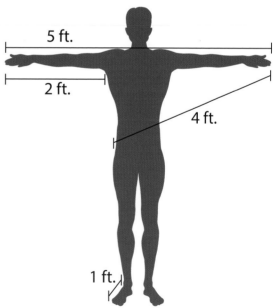

Paracord Wrap

Even if you are in a situation where you want to be camouflaged, it is a good idea to have some brightly colored material stored in your pack. The colors will stand out against nature's backdrop and will help you to be more visible to others if you need to be seen. You'll save time in finding a misplaced tool if there's a brightly colored lanyard tied to it. Wrapping paracord around tools works great for making a quick handle.

Here is an easy way to add a handle to a tool or to give it some extra grip. It is also a useful way to carry extra cordage that you can undo and use for something else.

1. Measure how long you want the handle to be. With one end of the paracord, make a loop so that the cut end of the paracord is on the bottom of the handle and the top of the loop will be where the handle ends.

Tips for the Outdoors

2. From the bottom of the handle, take the longer end of the paracord and begin tightly wrapping upward around the handle. As you wrap, try to keep the two strands from the loop straight and side by side.

3. Once the wrap gets close to the top, thread the paracord through the front side of the loop. Keep enough cord available to go through the loop. Be sure to keep everything tight as you near the end.

4. Depending on how tight the wrap is, this next step can be a bit difficult. The end of the cord that is hanging out of the bottom of the handle needs to be pulled straight down. This will close the loop at the top and cinch the paracord end upon itself. This might take some muscle and a better grip. Use the pliers on the Swiss Army Knife for a better grip, or, if there is enough cord, wrap it around the Swiss Army Knife and use it as a handle to pull the cord. While pulling the string it may be necessary to hold onto the handle wrap so that it doesn't slip too much. This will close the loop at the top.

5. Once the paracord has been cinched, the ends need to be cut and burned. Using the scissors, cut enough of the cord so that just a few centimeters remain, then use a lighter to heat the cut end. If too much is melted, it turns into a big blob of a mess. When the end is soft, I take the side of the lighter and press the melted end down and into the body of the wrap. This helps to adhere the cut end to the body of the wrap.

Keeping Your Mind Focused

There are many debates and arguments within the survival community regarding methodologies and gear. But I think that there is one thing that everyone in the community can agree on: the most important aspect of survival is the psychology of it, or the will to survive. In reading or talking to people, you may have heard of the survival pyramid. Think of a pyramid that is broken into three sections—top, middle, and bottom. The top represents the least important and the bottom is the most important. The top section is the smallest and contains your survival kit, gear, and supplies. The next-largest section is the middle, and it contains your knowledge. Last is the bottom, which is the largest section and contains your will to survive. It is a simple visual that I use to help people remember the hierarchy of what is important in a survival situation.

"Look deep into nature, and then you will understand everything better."
—Albert Einstein

SURVIVAL RULES OF THREE

You can survive

- **three minutes** without air.

- **three hours** (maintaining core temperature) without shelter.

- **three days** without water.

- **three weeks** without food.

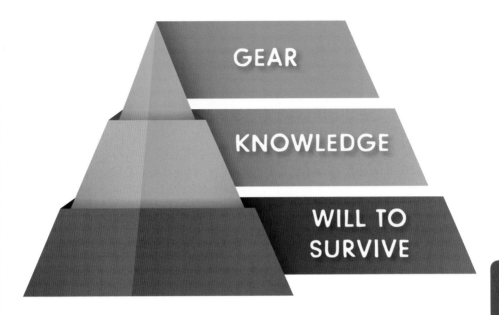

Your will to live outweighs all else in survival situations!

In an emergency situation, remind yourself of why you want to survive. This could mean thinking of loved ones or other meaningful aspects of your life. No matter how bad things are, look for an opportunity to take advantage of, and do your best to put a positive spin on a bad situation. If you can't sing, then whistle; if you can't whistle, then hum. Figuratively, this means there is more than one way to accomplish something, but this can also be taken literally. If you're all by yourself, why not sing, whistle, or hum? It can help you feel less tense.

Signaling and Navigation

Adventures in the wild don't always go according to plan. At some point you may find yourself disoriented and lost. There are many ways in which you can help others find you. Movement, color, and sound are your three best friends in nature when trying to be noticed.

Always pay attention to your surroundings. While it is important to look down and watch where you are stepping in the wild, it is equally important to look around so you can navigate your surroundings. This will help you notice and remember landmarks, as well as keep your bearing. Speaking of landmarks, it is important to look back after passing them, because landmarks can look very different from different angles. Knowing what a landmark looks like from different angles will help if you find yourself backtracking..

Use Landmarks

There have been many instances of people who were very close to a road or civilization but couldn't keep their bearing and ended up walking in circles. A good way to keep a bearing is to pick a prominent spot in front of you as well as behind you. Walk to the spot in front of you and stop. Look back to make sure you are still aligned in a straight line with the previous landmark. Now, pick a landmark that is in front of you and repeat this process as many times as necessary until you reach familiar ground.

"Leave the road, take the trails."
—Pythagoras

A fallen tree can be a noteworthy landmark.

Making a Compass

A compass will only help you if you know which direction you want to go or if you have a map. Having a map (a paper map won't lose battery power!), or at least some knowledge of the region you're in, is going to be needed, along with a compass. There are some Swiss Army Knife models and kits that come with a compass, so if you are fortunate enough to have one, you can skip this section. But what if you don't have one of those models or the compass breaks? In my case, I carry the SwissChamp, which doesn't have a compass. There is something else on the Champ that can help me though: a very small pin. I can turn that pin into a compass needle if I magnetize it. There are a couple ways to do this:

- Rubbing the pin several times through a piece of silk material will magnetize it.
- Rubbing the pin a few times in one direction along a magnet will also magnetize it.

Once the pin has been magnetized, place it on top of the smallest leaf you can find that will hold it and place that leaf in a puddle or a cup of water. If the pin is properly magnetized, it will begin to turn the leaf, much like the needle in a compass. When the pin stops, it will be displaying a north–south reading. I suggest doing this several times in order to make sure you are getting the best reading possible.

Making a Drafting Compass

A drafting compass can help in determining distances on a map, as well as serving other functions. Since I love to write and doodle, I always have three writing utensils on me: a wooden pencil, a pen, and a marker. These items should be in everyone's packs because they can be very useful. I suppose that is why Victorinox started including a ballpoint pen in some of their models.

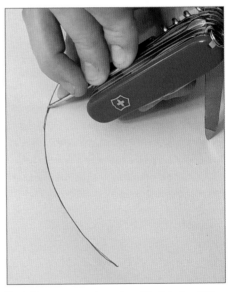

The drafting compass may be used even if the Swiss Army Knife doesn't come with a pen tool.

For models with a retractable pen, extend one of the tools on the Swiss Army Knife at an angle. Use the point of that tool to center the compass. The pen can then be used to draw arcs and circles and to measure distance.

If your model doesn't come with a pen but you have a writing utensil in your supplies, you can still make a drafting compass. Extend one of the tools to use as the other point. Attach the writing utensil to the frame of the Swiss Army Knife with cordage or tape and use as described above.

Signaling

USING A BRIGHT COLOR TO SIGNAL

A bright color is going to stand out against nature's neutral color scheme. If you're lost, you can hang your iconic red Swiss Army Knife from a tree limb or simply lay it out on a rock in an open area. Anyone who is glassing (using binoculars) the area is likely to notice this. Make sure that all of the tools of the knife are pulled out from the frame in order to produce more surface area that is reflective.

A reflective surface can be seen by a plane or other first responders from a very long distance. In the absence of a signaling mirror, the knife blade and other tools on the Swiss Army Knife can be used. Extend the knife blade and position it in the direction of the first responders and move the Swiss Army

Knife up and down so that it catches and reflects the sunlight. If the metal surfaces are severely scratched or dirty, sand and other grit can be used to polish the surface beforehand.

MARKING YOUR TRAIL (TRAILBLAZING)

Sometimes the best option may be to attempt self-rescue and walk out of a bad situation. If you do, mark the way in which you came and the direction in which you are going, just in case you become disoriented and backtrack,

Here is an additional method for trailblazing. Carry pieces of burned wood from your fire and use them as a marking tool on surfaces such as trees or rocks. One downside of this method is that the markings could be washed away by rain.

or if first responders come upon your path. Arrows or other marks can be cut into trees with the blade or any other appropriate tool contained in the Swiss Army Knife. Cutting pieces of fabric and hanging them from a tree will act as a marker flag. Breaking branches or thick vegetation is also a means of blazing a trail. Any kind of unnatural-looking marking will draw attention and increase your chances of being found.

LEAVING NOTES

Some of the Swiss Army Knife models come with a ballpoint pen. If writing material such as paper is available, then notes can be left along your path. Include information that pertains to the direction in which you are going and if you are in need of medical attention. Anchor the note by leaving it under a rock or piercing it with a branch.

A makeshift writing utensil can be easily made using fire. Find a branch and taper one end with the blade. Stick the end of the branch into the fire until it is sufficiently burned on the outside. The blackened end can then be used just like the tip of a pencil to mark or write on hard surfaces much like a kid does with sidewalk chalk.

USING SIGNAL FIRES

Signal fires should be placed in open areas and on high ground when possible, to ensure that the smoke and fire itself are highly

visible. Tree canopies will thin out a smoke column quite a bit, so make sure there is an open area above the fire. Also have plenty of fuel piled up next to the fire. This is especially important for the tinder, so that the fire can be ignited as quickly as possible. Use the magnifying glass or a ferrocerium rod with the Swiss Army Knife to start the fire (see the "Making Fire" section, page 82). When a good fire base has been created, burn green foliage to create a column of thick white smoke that will be highly visible.

Even a small pile of green foliage can produce a lot of white smoke.

SIGNAL MIRROR

What You Will Need

- **Aluminum soda can**
- **Knife or scissors**
- **Reamer**

ESTIMATED TIME FOR PROJECT

5–10 minutes

A signal mirror is a simple yet incredibly important piece of equipment. It is made of a reflective material with a hole in the center, and it is used to reflect sunlight toward a potential rescue party. This item is usually a staple in the packs of many outdoorsmen, but we can easily find ourselves in survival situations lacking ideal gear. Seek out trash to use as mirror material if needed. Sadly, human trash can be found even in some of the most remote areas of the world.

1. Make one long cut from the top of the can to the bottom. Use any tool on your Swiss Army Knife with a point on it to make a small hole in the side of an aluminum can. Then use the knife or scissors to cut out a small square or rectangular piece of metal.

2. Use the scissors to make a perpendicular cut at the top and bottom. After several inches have been cut, make the last cut from top to bottom to create a rectangular piece. I am going to be using the inside of the can, since we want a shiny, reflective surface. I will call this the front side since it will be the side pointed away from me when I am using it. On the back side, use the reamer or the knife blade to cut out a small circular hole in the center of the square piece. I recommend making the cut in this direction because it can produce small pieces of metal sticking outward. You don't want those pieces on the side you hold up close to your eye. Safety first, safety always!

3. Use the reamer to puncture a hole through the center of the aluminum. And just like that, a signal mirror is made!

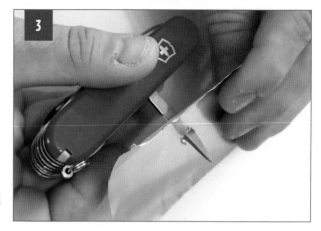

Now how does this thing work? Bring the mirror up to eye level so that you can look through it with one eye. With your other hand, make a V-shape with your index and middle finger and hold it out in front of you at arm's length. Move your outstretched hand so that the rescue party, boat, plane, helicopter, etc., are in between the V-shape of your fingers. Line up the mirror so that when you are looking through it you can see whom you are trying to signal. Now, move the mirror in an up-and-down motion so that you can see reflected sunlight moving up and down your hand and in between the V-shape. This will create a bright, flashing reflection that can be seen from a very long distance.

If the surface isn't as reflective as you like, you can brighten it with a little elbow grease. Natural materials such as dirt and sand can be used to polish the surface much like sandpaper does. This will work much better if you are by a water source to wash away the residue.

While this works best on bright sunny days, you may still get enough reflection to grab someone's attention.

A WORD OF ADVICE

The thin metal of the aluminum can is extremely sharp and can easily cut skin. Use extreme caution when working with it, and wear gloves if available.

WHISTLE

If you forgot to pack your signal whistle, don't fret. You can easily make one from natural materials. Cut a piece of wood that is at least the thickness of a pencil, then cut a notch in the top of the wood that will be where the sound comes out. Don't make this cut too deep at the beginning, just enough to create the shape. Create the mouthpiece by cutting the end of the branch at roughly a 45° angle.

Now remove the bark, but keep its tubular shape. Using the knife, cut into the bark all the way around the piece of wood, but try not to cut into the wood. Beat the bark off the wood. The frame of the Swiss Army Knife can be used for this, but it would be better to use another piece of wood. Gently, but firmly, beat on the bark all the way around the branch. This softens the under layer of the bark so that the outer layer can be removed. After hitting the outer layer for a bit, try to pull the bark off in one piece. Holding onto the bark, twist your hand back and forth while pulling it off.

Once the tube has come off, carefully place it to the side for future use. Using the knife, cut a thin layer from the top of the wood where the mouthpiece will be. This cut will form a small channel for the air to travel from the mouthpiece to the sound chamber. Cut out the rest of the sound chamber, but don't take out too much wood or there is a risk of the whistle snapping.

When all of the internal carving has been done, carefully twist and slide the bark tube back onto the whistle so that the sound chamber holes in the whistle and the bark line up. Achieving the desired sound can take some practice in carving out the sound chamber and the air channel correctly. When done right, it can produce a very loud whistle.

Alternate Method

There is a less labor-intensive method of creating a whistle. Using the knife and surgical precision, cut off a thick piece of grass from the surrounding vegetation. Insert the grass blade between the thumbs so it is being held by the tips and the base of the thumbs. Slightly rotate your thumbs inward toward your body to create a small channel, exposing the midsection of the grass. Bend the tips of your thumbs and use your knuckles as the mouthpiece in which to blow through. This was the whistle I learned to make and had used for much of my childhood.

Making Fire

Fire is one of mankind's oldest and most important tools. The ability to make it in an emergency situation cannot be overemphasized. You want to stay warm, cook food, boil water, make tools, keep animals and insects at bay, and signal for help—plus, I love all of the different ways that I can make a fire.

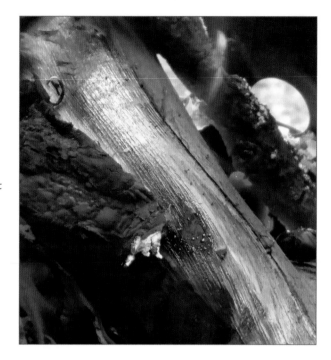

In My Experience

I attended a bonfire party in some farmer's field years ago. One of the kids was asked to get the fire going. He grabbed a green branch (fresh, with a lot of moisture in it) and held a lighter to the end of it. After a few minutes of watching this, I realized no one else was going to intervene, so I did. I explained to him why that green branch wasn't going to work. The kid could have used all of the fluid in the lighter can and still not have caught that branch on fire. In an emergency situation, resources like lighter fluid are precious and should be conserved at all costs.

Have you ever heard the saying "where there is smoke, there is fire"? That is not necessarily the case when you are trying to start a fire. If you have ever tried to make a fire using unconventional methods, you know what I am talking about. Here are some tips to remember:

- **Have patience.** Trying to create a fire with sparks, by friction, or even with a lighter is not always easy. Couple that with the circumstance in which you are trying to start a fire (you may be freezing, hungry, tired, etc.) and this task can quickly become beyond frustrating.

- **Always have enough burning material ready.** Once you have a flame, you don't want to scramble for more fuel. Have a large tinder bundle and a pile of kindling all set up. It takes a while for a large piece of wood to catch fire. The tinder and kindling will burn easily and help keep the fire going.

- **Don't suffocate the fire.** This combines the first two tips. Once a fire is started, you may become excited, lose your patience, and try to add too much fuel too quickly. In doing so, the fire can suffocate and die out. You must baby it at first and let it build on its own.

HELPFUL MODIFICATIONS

A small amount of cotton stored under the corkscrew can be used for fire-starting material. Since it compresses nicely, a whole cotton ball can be threaded directly onto the corkscrew.

A small amount of steel wool can be stored under the corkscrew. Steel wool paired with a battery makes for a great fire starter.

Always carry a fire-making kit. Making a fire can be difficult even in the best of conditions. And if the conditions are somewhat adverse, this task can turn impossible. Know that you may not get a fire going; don't waste too much energy and time in trying. Having a fire-making kit will greatly improve the odds of making fire.

I have found that the kits you can make at home are not only cheaper but work better than most store-bought kits. They can be as big or small as you want, and you can customize them as you see fit. Pictured below are items that should be included in your kit. If you have a belt holster for your Swiss Army Knife, you can fit a small fire kit inside of it as well. Fire kits should contain two types of items: a way in which to create a spark or a flame, and material to use as tinder.

Pictured left to right: UCO Stormproof matches with striker, magnesium shavings wrapped in duct tape, fatwood, cedar bark shavings, dryer lint, jute twine, ferrocerium rod, magnesium rod, and pieces of charcoal. Can you tell what is missing? Not pictured is the most obvious tool that should always be in a kit: a lighter.

The Foundation of Your Fire

Wood that is in direct contact with the ground is most likely going to be wet or damp, so always collect fuel that is off the ground. Tinder bundles and kindling are the foundation for creating fire. Tinder is usually more difficult to acquire than kindling because it needs to be a very fine and dry material (such as a bird's nest). In fact, if you can find a real bird's nest, you may even find some eggs for breakfast!

"Nature is pleased with simplicity. And nature is no dummy."
—Isaac Newton

If you can't find a nest, use the knife to peel dry bark shavings from branches. Take all of the shavings and smash them together in your hand; even roll it around like a dough ball. Use your thumbs to make a depression for the center. Kindling should be pieces of wood no thicker than your fingers. When you break a twig and it makes that distinct snapping sound, you know that it is very dry.

Another tool that works well for tinder is the wood saw. Normally the wood saw is used

Sawing downward works best with dry wood, but since there is so much surface area exposed in the shavings, green wood will work.

Fine wood dust burns very quickly, so make a big pile of it!

Making Fire

somewhat perpendicular to the wood so that it cuts into it. When making tinder, however, the wood saw needs to be placed almost parallel to the wood. Saw the upper layer of the wood in a downward fashion to create a fine wood dust.

This material is very helpful when placed in the center of a tinder bundle because it ignites very easily. Make sure to have something such as a piece of bark, leaf, or handkerchief beneath where you are cutting in order to collect the dust.

Here are the shavings I collected using the wood saw. Even though it was windy that day, I was able to light them with a single paper match.

Pictured left to right: tree bark for a bird's nest tinder bundle, SwissChamp, and kindling.

Firesticks are useful for maintaining an initial flame and for making the flame larger, especially in windy conditions. To make a firestick, take a branch and use the thumb-pushing method (see page 59) to cut progressively larger curls from the tip of the branch upward. This opens the wood, producing more surface area to burn. This feathering technique can also be used on wood matches to produce a larger flame. The small blade works well for this.

Use the thumb-pushing method to avoid cutting the feathered pieces off.

Feathering a match like the firestick will help to create a bigger flame. Be careful not to break the body of the match.

Making Fire

Four Ways to Create Fire

FERROCERIUM ROD

<table>
<tr><td>

What You Will Need

- **A ferrocerium rod**
- **Metal striker**
- **Tinder bundle**

ESTIMATED TIME FOR PROJECT

1 minute, with ideal conditions, materials, and experience

</td></tr>
</table>

A ferrocerium rod is a metal rod that produces sparks when scraped against another metal surface. Many outdoorsmen carry these on their person because they are long lasting and work even when they are wet. They come in various shapes and sizes.

The rods I use have a hole drilled in them so they can easily be attached to the key ring of the Swiss Army Knife or a length of paracord. Normally I would use the spine of a knife to scrape against the ferrocerium rod, but I don't recommend that with the Swiss Army Knife for two reasons. First, it's much harder to produce a lot of sparks with stainless steel. Second, because many of the blades on the Swiss Army Knife don't lock when open, the knife can snap shut on your

hand when applying downward pressure on the ferrocerium rod. For these reasons, I recommend using the metal saw as pictured below or using the spine of the metal saw. Place the ferrocerium rod so that the end is touching the tinder bundle. Use the spine or the metal saw itself to scrape hard and quickly to produce sparks. Once there is smoke, blow *softly and consistently* to help the ember grow until there is a flame.

The ferrocerium rod should actually be much closer to the tinder than pictured.

When the ferrocerium is positioned where it should be, the sparks you see in the picture will go into the center of the tinder bundle.

Making Fire

BOW DRILL

With friction fire-starting methods, your own energy can burn out quickly. Make sure you are in a comfortable position when attempting them to avoid further frustration.

Using a bow drill is a primitive yet effective way to start a fire. It also requires a lot of patience. As with most skills, I highly recommend that this particular method be practiced before it is actually needed. Even in a controlled environment (at home), I have had difficulty getting this method to work. This is one of those "make it or break it" methods. I have produced a smoking pile of dust within a minute or two, but I have also given up after an hour of trying.

Obtain a piece of wood for your bow. When possible, use a dry piece of wood. A green piece of wood will have some give to it, causing traction to be lost in the string.

Cut a notch on each end of the wood with the small or large blade of the Swiss Army Knife. Attach cordage (shoelaces, paracord, rope, etc.) to each end. There needs to be a very slight amount of slack in the cord so that it can be wrapped around the drill.

Use the knife tool to taper one end of a piece of hardwood for the spindle. Rounding out the top end of the drill that will be resting in the handle will help the drill to spin easier. Cut a V-shaped notch into the end of the softwood using the wood saw. Just above the notch, use the tip of the blade to cut a small hole into the wood where the end of the drill rests. Cutting the slot just under the drill mark will allow proper airflow to the wood as it is heated and create a channel for the dust to be collected.

Make one loop around the spindle with the cordage by twisting the spindle around the cordage. Use a rock, cup, or other piece of wood as a handle on top of the spindle in order to hold it. The handle needs to have a hole or small depression for the spindle to rest in. Lubricating the inside of the handle will help reduce friction between the handle and the top of the drill. Lip balm, petroleum jelly, oil, or animal fat could be used to lubricate the inside of the handle. Make sure that there is a dry platform below the plank to keep it away from moisture. A piece of bark works well for this. If the temperature outside is comfortable, use your bare feet to hold down the plank to prevent moisture from your shoes or socks from interfering.

Kneel and place your foot a few inches away from where the spindle will be drilling into the plank. Then rest the arm holding the handle onto your leg. Move the bow in a back and forward motion to turn the spindle while exerting downward pressure on the spindle handle. Getting the feel for this will take a little bit of practice, but you will soon find a rhythm. A fine dust will be created that, when hot enough, will start to smoke. Don't stop once you see smoke—keep going! The smoke that you first see is coming from the friction of the wood and not the dust burning on its own.

Once you see smoke, continue to drill for roughly another thirty seconds to build up the dust pile. After the hot dust has been smoking on its own for about a minute, it can be gently transferred to the center of a tinder bundle. Without crushing the hot dust, fold the tinder bundle in half and begin blowing into the center to create a bigger ember.

A WORD OF ADVICE

The smoking wood dust is very fine and can easily be put out. Before transferring it, don't blow directly onto it. Instead, wave your hand back and forth over the pile to give it a little bit of air.

Making Fire

MAGNIFYING GLASS

A piece of burned material such as char cloth or charcoal will create an ember much quicker with this method and should be placed in the middle of the tinder bundle.

A magnifying glass was my favorite way to start a fire when I was a boy (to be honest, it still is). This method can work very quickly and requires almost zero physical exertion, but it relies on the good fortune of having a sunny day. The best time to use a magnifying glass for this purpose is midday when the sun is at its zenith.

Angle the magnifying glass so that there is the smallest point of sunlight in the tinder bundle. Wear sunglasses if you have them, as staring at the bright focal point can mess with your eyes. The intensity of the sun, fire-starting materials, and the magnification of the lenses will all play a role in how quickly this method will work. Using the magnifying glass on my SwissChamp and a piece of charcoal, I produced a glowing ember in thirty seconds. There have also been times when it has taken much longer because the clouds were not cooperating. Once there is smoke, blow softly and consistently to help the ember grow until there is a flame within the tinder bundle.

A WORD OF ADVICE

Dust on the magnifying glass will greatly reduce its ability to produce fire. Wipe both sides clean before trying to use it.

FIRE PLOW

The fire plow is a friction method for starting a fire and is probably the most labor-intensive method there is. You are literally going to be rubbing two pieces of wood together in order to create fire. So roll up your sleeves and let's create fire—caveman style!

1. You'll need two pieces of wood. The first piece should be as flat as possible, because it is going to act as the base. Ideally, it should be made from a softwood. The second piece needs to be a straight, round branch. Ideally, this piece should be made from a hardwood. Start making the groove by cutting an outline with the knife blade.

2. Prepare the base. Lay the board on the ground and use the chisel tool on the Swiss Army Knife to cut a small groove down the center of the wood. If your Swiss Army Knife doesn't have the chisel tool, the knife can be used to achieve the same result, but using the chisel saves the tip of the knife blade and is safer. Don't worry about making the groove smooth with the chisel.

3. This groove is where the hardwood branch will be "plowed" back and forth to create friction. Prepare the hardwood branch by using the knife to cut one end into a point. The tip doesn't need to have a fine point. It only needs to be small enough to fit inside the groove of the baseboard.

4. Place some green vegetation or a bandana around the uncut end of the branch to act as padding for your hand as you move the branch back and forth. Position the padded end of the branch into the palm of one hand and place your other hand about midway down the branch. Keep the baseboard from moving by stepping or kneeling on the end closest to you. Work the branch back and forth through the groove with steady downward pressure. As you can see, the groove is not that long, just a few inches. You want to keep strokes fairly short, as longer strokes will require more effort due to heat loss. As the two pieces are rubbed together, tinder will be created as a fine dust at the end of the base.

Making Fire

5. End the stroke with the tip of the branch just touching the pile of dust, without knocking the dust off the wood. It may take several attempts to get this, but with some practice you will soon find your "groove." Once enough dust has been collected and enough heat generated, a small ember will be created in the pile. You may not be able to see the ember, but you will know that it is there when the tinder is smoking on its own. Transfer the ember to another tinder pile and gently blow on it until you have a flame.

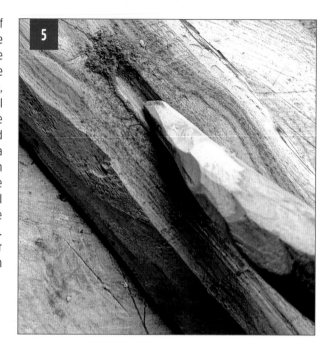

A WORD OF ADVICE

With friction fire-starting methods, your energy can burn out quickly. Start out slow and steady at first to warm the wood up, then increase your speed and pressure. As the wood blackens and you see smoke, continue for at least another fifteen seconds. When you stop, if you don't see smoke rising from the pile of dust, jump right back into working the groove before everything cools down.

MAKING A HEAT REFLECTOR

This is a very small heat reflector wall with the Hercules model standing guard.

If you need to spend an extended amount of time in one location, it would be worthwhile to build a wall that will act as a heat reflector for the fire. This simple wall will help direct heat back toward your shelter instead of dispersed into the air and lost. The wall should be placed a few feet away from the fire.

Obtain four pieces of wood that will be the poles for the frame. Cut them to equal length with the wood saw. Pull out the large blade to create points on one end of all four poles—they don't have to be perfect. Pound the four poles into the ground, leaving a gap between them.

Roughly measure the length and width between the poles. Simply use another branch or a length of cordage as a measuring stick. Use these dimensions to determine the size of the logs to be cut in order to fill in the gap. Once the logs have been collected, stack them horizontally to fill in the gap of the poles. The longer and taller you can build these, the better they will work. Generally I aim to make these at least 4 feet (122cm) long and 4 feet (122cm) high, but don't hurt yourself trying to carry a log that is too big. If the weight of the wall begins pushing the poles outward, close the top of the poles by tying them together; this will help to hold the stack together.

Making Fire

MAKING CHAR CLOTH

Char cloth is made of material that is 100% cotton, linen, or jute. After this cloth is charred, it creates a material that takes a spark extremely well. When making your own, use old underwear, socks, or T-shirts that are 100% cotton.

Puncture a hole in the lid of a metal container with the reamer tool. For this batch I used the scissors to cut small patches from an old towel. Place a few layers of material in the container and replace the lid.

Put the container onto or next to a fire, and watch it carefully so that the material doesn't "cook" for too long. Smoke will begin to billow out of the hole in the lid—this is perfectly normal. Once the smoke stops, take the container away from the heat source and check it. The material should be charred black all the way through. If some of the material is still the original color or brown, put it back on the fire for a few moments.

Once the material is blackened all the way through, it is ready to be used. Use a ferrocerium rod to create a spark or use the magnifying glass on the Swiss Army Knife to easily create an ember on the char cloth. Place the ember into a tinder bundle, and there you have it!

Using a few layers of fabric, as shown in the picture, took around five minutes to blacken. Making char cloth is very useful and is why I like to carry two metal tins on my back.

Transporting Fire

You went through all the hard work of getting a fire started and keeping it going, but what do you do when it is time to break camp and move on? When you extinguish your fire—and you should *always* extinguish your fire—it's best to smother it. Using water is not a good idea because it may be in short supply. Water causes the fire to billow a lot—that is, it gives off a lot of smoke. Piling dirt on the fire is the quickest and easiest way to put it out.

But there is a way in which you can carry fire with you so that you don't have to spend so much time starting another one. Grab a piece of punky wood (wood that is soft and crumbly, caused by rotting). Use the knife to dig out a depression in the wood. Before extinguishing your fire, place a hot coal from the fire in the hole of the punky wood. The punky wood will smolder instead of burn, allowing you to carry a hot coal with you. This will save you time and energy when you get to your next location. When you are ready to start another fire, simply add some tinder to the ember in the wood.

A second method of transporting fire is to make a torch like those used by angry villagers (see the next page).

Make sure that the punky wood is smoldering and ready to transport before putting out the fire.

MAKING A TORCH

A torch can be a valuable asset because of the many things it can offer. It can provide light, help transport fire, keep wild animals and insects at bay, and offer a means of signaling for help should you require rescue. When building a torch, think of it as a big candle. You need a handle in which to carry it, a fuel source that will burn, and a wick that helps to contain the fuel source.

METHOD 1

The first method is very easy to make, but the fuel source may not be readily available. With both methods you need the torch handle to be made of green wood so that it doesn't burn easily. The torch handle should be about 4 feet (122cm) long so that you can hold it away from your body. Use the wood saw to cut a branch to the proper length. Use the knife to cut a piece of material (ideally 100% cotton) to wrap around the end of the torch and use as a wick. A synthetic material won't work as well because it won't absorb the fuel very effectively, and the synthetic material has a tendency to melt. The material should be soaked in a flammable liquid. To avoid getting any of the fuel on your hands, wrap the end of the torch with the material first, then apply the fuel. Any liquid that is flammable should work just fine. Take an

This torch was very quick to make. It consists of layers of twigs and cedar bark. The end of the wood was split into four prongs using the baton method, so that material can be placed and held inside.

ignition source, such as a lighter or a twig that is on fire, to ignite the end of the torch. Depending on the fuel source that is being used, the torch should burn for about fifteen to twenty minutes.

METHOD 2

The second method is a little more involved but very effective. Find a piece of green wood that is roughly 4 feet (122cm) in length. Split one end into quarters using the baton method of cutting (see page 61). Take two pieces of wood and insert them in between the cuts to keep the quarters separated. Find a natural source of fuel, such as pine resin, and a wick, such as a pine cone, cattail, extra clothing you may have, a large piece of punky wood, or a thickly wrapped bundle of bark shavings.

Pine resin can be found on a tree where it has been damaged. The tree secretes the resin as a barrier against insects and anything that could cause the tree to become diseased. Use the large blade to cut and scrape the resin into a container. I like to be environmentally conscious as much as I can when collecting natural materials. Only take what you need, and leave a layer of resin on the tree.

The resin can be used in two different ways. It can be used as is and smeared all over the wick, or it can be heated into a liquid. The torch seems to burn a bit longer if the resin is liquefied because it is integrated more

into the wick. To liquefy the resin, place it in a container and heat it gradually next to a fire. Do not place the container of resin into the fire or the resin may catch fire. When the resin has melted, pour the resin over the wick until it is soaked. Place the wick inside the quartered section of the handle. Take out the pieces of wood that were holding the quartered sections open so that those sections will tighten a bit and hold the wick. From here, simply light the wick and the torch should burn for ten to fifteen minutes.

If resin or a flammable liquid is not available, the torch head can be tightly packed with any material that will burn, such as bark, wood shavings, cattails, dry foliage, etc. The torch will then have a much quicker burn time.

A WORD OF CAUTION

Burning pieces will fall off the torch. Always be mindful of your surroundings when carrying a torch, especially when walking through very dry country. You don't want to accidentally start a larger fire that could burn out of control. To avoid injury, always hold the torch out in front of you, and do not hold it straight up and down.

Campsite

At the end of the day, you want to make sure that there is still plenty of daylight left in order to locate a proper location for shelter and to set that shelter up. A shelter is going to help protect you from the elements and give you a better night's sleep by providing a comfortable place to rest. It is important that there is daylight when surveying a campsite so that you can identify any possible dangers of that location.

Avoid setting up camp too close to a river or stream due to rising water levels. Also avoid ravines in flash-flood areas. Always remember to look up and stay away from widow-makers. *Widow-makers* is the common term for large, broken tree branches that are still hanging onto a tree and could fall down at any time. I use this expression for anything that could fall on you, so the same is true for rocks along a rock wall.

I will look down and inspect the ground as well for signs of fallen materials, poisonous plants, small animal dens, and even an excess number of insects. I remember waking up once when camping and feeling itchy all over.

I hadn't noticed a huge ant colony that wasn't far from where I decided to bed down for the night.

Avoid wandering around in the dark, which is very dangerous even with a flashlight. So gather material for a fire and create that fire before it gets dark. We already know how to use Swiss Army Knives to start a fire, so let's see what they can do to help with shelters.

Shelters

Shelters don't have to be elaborate structures unless an extended amount of time is being spent in one location. Sometimes simple shelters can be better. They only need to be big enough for you to comfortably lie down in.

Do not lay directly on the ground, as you will lose a lot of body heat and run the risk of becoming wet. Using the saw or knife, cut wood, bark, or grass that you can lie down on to create a layer between you and the ground. Dead air space is one of the best insulators. As uncomfortable as it may be, even a layer of small logs or branches will help.

> *"I believe that there is a subtle magnetism in Nature, which, if we unconsciously yield to it, will direct us aright."*
> —Henry David Thoreau

When using a tarp or canvas, you may need a few stakes to secure the ends of the tarp. Using the knife, taper one piece of wood into a spear point. Take a rock or another larger piece of wood to pound the stake into the ground at a slight angle. It is a good idea to cut a shallow notch into the stake to prevent the cordage from slipping off. Hang the tarp at a steep angle to allow rain and snow to run off.

To save time and energy, make use of natural structures such as a large log or a fallen tree. When using a downed tree or log, you may only need to shore up the sides and add a roof. Sometimes a simple lean-to made from branches will be enough to get you through the night.

When rain proofing a shelter, always overlap the material as you start from the bottom and work your way up so that the top layers overlap the preceding layers. This pattern allows water to run off the roof and sides rather than find its way into the shelter. The wood saw works great for cutting many smaller branches with an abundance of leaves that can be used as shingles. When making a lean-to, the cuts of wood don't have to be precise, but the wood saw and knife do help to make those cuts and make the shelter come together nicely.

If there is a depression or hole in the ground that is large enough to lay in, a simple shelter can be made by placing logs or branches over the top of it. Don't lay below ground level if there is a chance of rainfall.

If you have a tent, the Swiss Army Knife can help to create stakes, pull a stuck zipper flap, repair any holes or damages to the fabric of the tent, and create extra ventilation if needed.

Camp Security

There are a many things that the Swiss Army Knife can do to help beef up your camp security. The kind of security measures you may want to implement is dictated by the amount of time being spent in a single location and the possibility of dangers such as wild animals. A perimeter alarm system is going to take the least amount of time to set up. It will give you advance warning when something is trying to enter your camp.

Always keep an eye out for resources. Along your journey you may come across some metal containers, like soup or soda cans. Be sure to pick them up, because you can use them for your camp security. Metal containers, a long piece of cordage, and some rocks are the three ingredients for making an outdoor alarm system.

Using the reamer or punch tool, create two holes in the side of the can near the top but on opposite sides of one another. Next, drop several small stones into the cans. Thread the cordage through the holes. Repeat this process for as many cans as you have—the more the better! Hang the bundle of cans over a branch so that they are about 1 foot (30cm) lower than the branch. Bring the rest of the cordage down and begin weaving through the trees and vegetation about 1 foot (30cm) above the ground—this will be the "trip wire." When you get to the end of the cordage, anchor it to a tree trunk or other heavy object. When an animal walks across the path of the trip wire, it will move the line and cause the cans to bounce around. With the cans hitting themselves and the rocks inside, it should make a very distinct noise. Because you want this to be an advance warning system, set it about 30 to 40 yards (27–37m) away from where you'll be sleeping. If it is too close, you will not have enough time to react. If it is too far away, you may not hear the alarm.

Long-term survival in one location may require defenses that are a little more substantial, some might even say a little medieval. In the "Making Fire" section I talked about how to make a heat-reflecting wall. The same building technique and materials in that section can be used to create a wall around your camp. The wall will also act as a great wind breaker. Increase the size and length of the posts and logs to fill in the wall and make it more robust.

If security from large animals is of great concern, an added layer of protection can be added on the outside of the wall. Creating a

The reamer or punch can be used to make holes in the top of the cans. Use whatever cordage is available to string them up over a tree branch.

barrier of spiked branches should help deter any curious animals coming to your camp. Pick out branches or logs that are at least 1 inch (2.5cm) in diameter. With the knife, remove wood from one end to make a spear point. Pound the spear point into the ground at an angle; this needs to be well anchored into the ground. On the end of the branch that is now sticking out, carve another spear

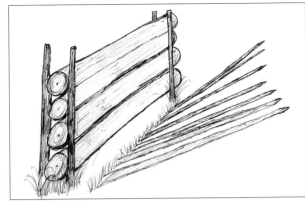

Adding a layer of thorny vegetation around the wall will further deter curious animals.

point. Making as many of these as you can, place them at different heights and angles to maximize the effectiveness of the barrier.

Campsite Tools

Being productive and finding ways to continuously improve your situation is key to surviving hard times. But this can be frustrating when we don't have the tools that we need. The Swiss Army Knife is certainly the mini toolbox that you are going to want in your pocket, but it is not always going to have everything you may need or want. Looking at different cultures, past and present, we can learn what basic tools are most important for our daily needs. Items like fishing hooks, nets, and containers are just some of the things that will greatly aid in a survival situation. Unfortunately,

these items are not packed away in the deep recesses of the Swiss Army Knife like some super spy gadget. However, with the variety of functions that the Swiss Army Knife offers, we can make an assortment of tools that will help us to survive and provide some creature comforts.

CORDAGE

What You Will Need

- **Tree bark** (I used cedar bark in project)
- **Knife blade**

ESTIMATED TIME FOR PROJECT

20 minutes (but varies depending on the amount of cordage you want)

In all of your supplies there are a handful of items that are invaluable because of the array of uses they can be used for, and cordage is one of those items. Listing all of the ways in which cordage can be used could probably fill up the rest of this book, but here is a short list:

- Handles
- Shelter construction
- Raft construction
- Making shoes
- Hoisting
- Making traps
- Slings
- Straps

There are a lot of natural materials that can be used to make cordage, such as grasses, vines, and tree bark. In my example, I am using the inner white layer of cedar bark because it is extremely strong. If you are being environmentally conscious when harvesting tree bark, only take it from one side. A tree can heal itself from many injuries, but if a cut is made that goes all the way around the trunk, the tree will certainly die.

I used the large blade to cut these small strips from the trunk of the tree. Depending on the size of cordage you want to make, you may want to cut considerably longer strips. Once the initial cuts are made, the inner white layer easily pulls away from the tree. The outer bark will need to be removed. If time is not an issue, soaking the pieces in water will help to remove unwanted bark.

The small knife offers the best control when attempting to make small cuts.

The traditional way of doing this is to let the white layer dry out for a few days before braiding, otherwise the cordage will shrink. Due to my lack of patience, I have always braided the material wet with no real problem in performance. Use the small blade to cut the individual strips to be used in the braiding process.

I normally cut the width of my strips under ¼ inch (6mm), but for demonstration purposes the largest piece is closer to ½ inch (13mm).

There are several different ways to braid cordage, but I like the weaving style pictured above. It uses three individual pieces that are passed back and forth over one another. This gives a thicker-diameter cordage, which works well for straps, handles, and general-purpose rope lines. The thinner the strands are, the easier it will be to weave or braid. Light hammering will help to separate the white material into thinner stands.

Here is a method for making longer lengths of cordage from the shorter strands. Take a piece of the inner bark and fold it in half. Tie an overhand knot at the top where the strand bends. Twist one strand several times before wrapping it around the other strand. Take the other strand and twist it, then wrap it around. Repeat this process until you get close to the end of the strand. Bring in a fresh piece of inner bark and twist it around the short strand. Continue the twisting and wrapping until the cordage is as long as you would like it to be. When you get to the end, tie an overhand knot to keep the cordage from unraveling.

A WORD OF ADVICE

Always make more cordage than you think you will need, because you can never have enough cordage!

Campsite

POLE HOOK

The convenience of a pole hook can save time and energy and be a safer means of reaching objects. Although a simple tool, it can be very useful in survival situations. It can be used to grab onto a branch with fruit and bring it down to be picked. A water bottle can be attached to the end and lowered to a watering hole that might be hard to reach. Use it to reach into thick, dangerous vegetation in order to pull out useful resources. It could also be used to help pull you up a steep hill, but be careful because the bindings may not take all of your weight.

This can be made from either one or two pieces depending on what you can find. Locate a branch that is roughly 6 feet (2m) long, or as long as the situation calls for. This can be made from one piece if there is a side branch thick enough to form

If you can't find a branch with a Y in it to cut with the wood saw, you can make this out of two separate pieces. In the photo, I used two pieces of wood connected with jute twine.

the hook at the end of the pole. If there is, use the wood saw to cut the wood just beyond the side branch. Use the knife to trim and shape the hook.

Making the pole from two separate pieces doesn't require much more work but will require the addition of cordage. Locate a pole as described above and a separate forked branch for the hook. Place the forked branch on top of the pole with the hook pointed out to the side. Tie the two pieces together with cordage.

In My Experience

Years ago I was hiking in an extremely hilly wooded area. To one side of me was a sapling with a thick side branch in the shape of a hook. I used my knife to cut the sapling down and make a pole hook. By using the pole hook to grab onto anything ahead of me, I was able to progress up the hills much quicker and without as much energy.

What would make a hike up a steep incline easier?

Campsite

ALUMINUM CAN CANDLE HOLDER

What You Will Need

- **Aluminum soda can**
- **Knife**
- **Scissors**

ESTIMATED TIME FOR PROJECT

5 minutes

Many people will carry what are called tea candles in their packs because they are incredibly small but useful. Even though these candles are quite small, in the right conditions they can be used for cooking, lighting, and even for warming up small enclosed spaces. One problem with keeping candles lit outdoors is competing against wind and rain. An aluminum can will help protect the candle from these elements.

1. On most soda cans there is a small curve on the top and bottom of the side of the can. Use the Swiss Army Knife to make a single cut down the side of the can between these two curves.

2. Make four more cuts: two on the top and two on the bottom. The cuts need to be perpendicular to the first cut and should be a few inches long, as large or small as you like.

3. Use these cuts to make a small door. Here, one door has been cut. The project could stop here, and the holder would still function pretty much the same. I like having two doors because I think it provides a bit more outward reflection. Use the knife to pry the two pieces away from each other. Once they are pulled apart, they should stay open on their own and a small tea candle can be placed within the can. The doors of the can may be opened or closed as much as you want by gently bending the aluminum.

4. Repeat the preceding cutting process, but in the opposite direction to create the other door.

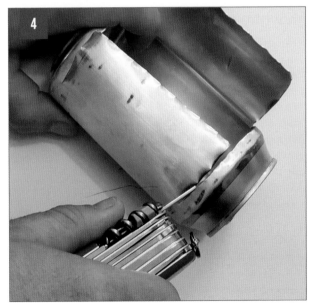

5. The holder is done; all that we need now is to insert a candle. I like to carry small emergency candles in my pack and vehicle. They are slightly larger than traditional tea candles, but they last much longer. The one being used in the photo lasts up to nine hours!

6. Because the inside of the can is reflective, the can may be used as a small lantern. Keeping the doors open should provide a bit more light than using the candle by itself.

A WORD OF ADVICE

The thin aluminum of the can heats up pretty quickly. Don't try to move it with your bare hands! Have the pop tab on top sticking straight up so it can be lifted using the hook or pliers on your Swiss Army Knife.

PINE PITCH GLUE

What You Will Need

- **Knife**
- **Stick**
- **Metal container**
- **Coals from a fire**

ESTIMATED TIME FOR PROJECT

30 minutes

Instant glue is great to add to your pack because it can temporarily fix many items quickly. But many people don't carry glue into the wild. It's a good thing that there is a natural way to make glue that has been used for eons. Other than being great for fire starting, the resin in pine trees can be used as a glue and as a means for waterproofing. This material is called pine pitch.

First you must locate a pine tree that has sustained a wound. When a pine tree is damaged, it protects and heals itself by secreting resin to cover the injured site. Over time the resin will harden. When gathering resin, the "fresher" (softer) it is, the better it will work. Sometimes you may not have a choice of freshness, so once you have found a tree with resin, use the knife of the Swiss Army Knife to cut

Natural glue source.

some of it off. Collect the resin by placing it into a container so that afterward it can be heated by fire and melted.

The best way to melt the resin is to start a fire and let it burn down to coals. There are two reasons for this. First, resin is very flammable and you do not want to heat it with flames dancing around the can. Second, you do not want to overcook the resin by using too much heat; you simply want to melt it into a goo. Periodically, use a stick to stir the resin as it melts, and be careful not to boil it.

Once most of the resin has been melted, add a secondary medium so that it is easier to work with and doesn't become too brittle once it hardens. While there are a couple of ingredients you could use for this step, the easiest would be coal from your fire. Collect some pieces of coal and crush them into a powder with a stick or a rock. Stir the powdered coal into the melted goo so that the mixture is uniform. As the resin begins to solidify, it can be wrapped around the stirring stick to create a glue stick. This glue stick can then be carried along with you.

When you need it, simply reheat the resin and apply the soft, melted material where needed. Allow it to dry and re-harden. This can be used to cover and waterproof small holes in gear, as well as to glue together pieces of tools that you make.

GARROTE

What You Will Need

- **Two pieces of wood for the handles**
- **Length of cordage**
- **Knife**
- **Wood saw**
- **Reamer**

ESTIMATED TIME FOR PROJECT

30 minutes

While the traditional use of a garrote is a bit grisly, it can come in handy for more practical uses. It can be used to help drag logs or bundles of wood, lift objects, hoist yourself up into a tree—as well as climb a tree—and a host of other applications. I have used a garrote many times. By looping the cordage around an object, one of the handles can be quickly cinched under the cordage in order to hold onto that item.

Find two pieces of wood that are as close in shape and size as possible. These will be the handles, so they need to fit comfortably in your hand. Use the wood saw to cut the pieces to the proper length and the knife to smooth out any imperfections on the surface of the wood. Next, use the reamer to drill a hole in the center of each handle. Thread one end of the cordage through the hole and tie the end into a knot so that the cordage

doesn't slip back through the hole. Repeat this step for the opposite end of the cordage and remaining handle.

Threading paracord through holes is easier if the ends are melted so that they don't fray. When using cordage with holes or notches in wood, round off the edges of the wood to prevent the cordage from fraying because of friction with the wood. Use the reamer or the tip of the knife to carve away the top layer around the hole in order to round it off.

The garrote is a simple tool with a variety of functions and is especially useful for carrying items.

A WORD OF ADVICE

If you happen to come across an abrasive wire, you can use the handles from this project to make a wire saw for cutting wood. This technique can also be used to repair broken handles on a wire saw you may already have.

Campsite

GRAPPLING HOOK

A makeshift grappling hook won't hold your weight—trust me, I have tried—but it still comes in quite handy. It can help in heaving rope lines into trees, hanging items from them, retrieving dropped items, bringing down a bird's nest for fire tinder, and trolling through water to obtain materials such as driftwood, aquatic plants, or anything else you may want to grab onto.

Pictured here is a simple two-pronged grappling hook. Cut three pieces of wood using the wood saw in your Swiss Army Knife. The larger piece will act as the frame to which the hooks will be tied as a foundation. Sharpen the ends of two smaller pieces of wood with the large or small blade. Hold the sharpened pieces to the frame at an angle and begin wrapping over and under with cordage to secure the pieces to the frame. If you have the time, use the reamer tool to drill a hole through the handle. This will give you a spot to thread and tie off one end of your cordage.

As you can see from the size of the two spear points, this grappling hook is going to be on the small end.

The grappling hook can also be used to raise and lower supplies off the ground.

MALLET (WOOD HAMMER)

What You Will Need

- **A large-diameter piece of wood** (hardwood would be best)
- **Wood saw**
- **Knife**

ESTIMATED TIME FOR PROJECT

30–45 minutes, but depends on the size of the mallet

A hammer can help in setting up a shelter or traps, cracking open food sources, and an array of other functions. While just grabbing a small log and using it like a hammer, sometimes it is better to have form meet function. Never use your Swiss Army Knife as a hammer; make this mallet instead.

Decide on a piece of wood that is right for you in terms of weight. Don't make it too heavy or too light. Mark off a section that will be the striking surface. Under this mark, use the wood saw to make a cut all the way around the log. The depth of this cut is going to depend on the diameter of the log being used.

Stand the log upright on a surface so that the striking surface is down and the handle end is pointing up. Extend the large knife and use the baton method (page 61) to cut downward along the edge. Once the knife

reaches the saw cut made previously, the piece of wood will fall off. Continue removing wood in this fashion until the desired size of the handle is made. From here the knife can be used to further shape and smooth out the handle. This can be one of those nice whittling projects done around the campfire.

Having a smaller handle will make your pounding experience much more comfortable and safer. With the Hercules, I was able to rough out the end in about twenty minutes, but I took the time to make the handle nice and smooth.

Campsite

PART 3: USING YOUR KNIFE IN THE WILD   **117**

DRILL

There are times when you'll want to make holes in a piece of wood. This is especially true for hand tools so that you can insert cordage for hanging purposes, or so that you don't drop the tool when in use. Typically you can use the reamer or the tip of the knife to "drill" a hole. Those tools work very well, but there are times when you'll want something that is a little smoother to use and possibly a different-sized hole than the tools can provide. It is time to look down at the ground and start searching for a pointy rock and a stick. Make sure the stick is as straight as possible.

After finding the materials, extend the knife blade and use the baton cutting method (page 61) to split one end of the stick. Insert the rock into the cut and bind it by wrapping

cordage around the end of the stick. In the fire-making section, there is a bow drill project (page 90). Familiarize yourself with that project, because you are going to need a bow and a handle for the drill. Insert the drill into the bow cordage as described in the bow drill project, and place the handle on top of the drill. Move the bow in a back and forth motion to spin the drill.

This rock drill was made with the Spartan model.

BARK CONTAINER

What You Will Need

- **Wood saw**
- **Knife**
- **Section of a log**
- **Cordage**

ESTIMATED TIME FOR PROJECT

30 minutes

When foraging for supplies like nuts and berries, you won't always have enough pockets in which to put them. (It's also hard getting berry stains out of clothes!) If you know your trees, choose one that releases its bark easily, like a birch tree. Birch is ideal because the bark can be peeled off with your hands, but other barks can be used.

Determine the size of the container and mark the dimensions on the log. Using a wood saw, cut the log a few inches (centimeters) beyond the marks. Saw off the ends of the log so they are roughly 1 inch (2.5cm) thick, and keep the two pieces. With the knife, cut a straight line down the length of the bark and peel it away from the log in one piece. This can be tricky, so take your time.

Once the bark has been removed, take one of the 1 inch (2.5cm)-thick log ends and wrap it in the bark so that it forms the end of the container. The original long cut into the bark will be the top of the container. Attach the bark to the wood with cordage. Repeat this process for the other end of the container. Finally, use the knife to create a larger opening in the top of the container. To make the container easier to carry, take some cordage and make a shoulder strap. When I was sporting this around, my wife nicknamed it the woodman's purse.

I had some trouble getting this bark off in one piece, but by overlapping the pieces it can still be used. A combination of paracord inner strands and jute twine was used to secure the ends and make a carrying strap.

Campsite

PACK

You may find yourself without a pack. Perhaps it was lost, damaged beyond repair, or eaten by a bear. In any case, making a pack frame is going to be helpful for carrying supplies. There are a variety of designs and materials you can use to make a pack, but I'm going to concentrate on two basic layouts.

Pack 1

The first pack is the quickest and easiest to construct. Use the wood saw to cut three pieces of wood. Lay out the pieces in the shape of a triangle with the ends overlapping one another. Secure the overlapping ends to one another with lengths of cordage. The tip of the triangle will be the top of the pack. To create carrying straps, tie a piece of cordage to the bottom of the frame and one of the side bars, creating a loop that can be slung over the shoulder. Repeat this for the other side so that there are two straps. This makes for a very thin profile pack that is easy to carry.

Pack 2

The second pack will take a little more time and materials to construct but will be able to carry more items. Take two limbs and form an L shape with overlapping ends. Secure them together with cordage. Make two of these, as they will form the sides of the pack. Secure two more crossbars, one at the end of the L shape and one at the top. Two more pieces will be needed that span between the end of the L to the top of the frame. This is the frame in the most basic form and could be used as is, but adding more branches as crossbars will help to support the pack. Use cordage to create straps as mentioned above.

With two straps, this improvised pack can be carried just like a backpack. To carry supplies, simply tie them to the frame of the pack.

PART 3: USING YOUR KNIFE IN THE WILD

IMPROVISED SUNGLASSES OR SNOW GOGGLES

What You Will Need

- **Material to cover your eyes**
- **Knife or scissors**
- **Cordage**

ESTIMATED TIME FOR PROJECT

15 minutes

Sunglasses offer more than just a great fashion statement. They offer UV protection from the sun and protection from physical objects, and they also reduce eyestrain. To reduce the possibility of sun blindness in extremely bright environments, improvised sunglasses can be made from a variety of materials. A soft, durable material, such as leather, would be ideal, but they can be made from just about anything: tree bark, cardboard, wood, or even an article of clothing. Cut two small slits in the material in which to see through. These small slits allow you to see while limiting the amount of light entering your eye.

Cardboard is not ideal, but I decided to use it because it was the first material that I found on my hike. As long as the material covers your eyes, the dimensions are not critical.

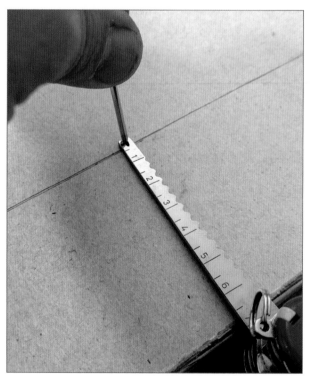

The hook disgorger holds the tip of the pen securely and ensures a straight line every time.

Draw a straight line all the way across the cardboard. Use the ballpoint pen, fish scaler, and a straight surface, such as a table edge, to accomplish this. With the fish scaler extended, place the end of the Swiss Army Knife flush with a straight surface. Having the bottle opener perpendicular will also help in keeping a line straight. The tip of the ballpoint pen should sit between the points of the hook disgorger so that, as you move the Swiss Army Knife along the edge, the pen will draw a straight line. (Drawing a line like this is not necessary for this project, but I wanted to share another way to use a tool.)

Use the scissors to cut along the line and the small knife to rough out some eye slits. On both ends of the material, use the reamer to poke little holes through the cardboard. Thread some cordage through the two holes, but only tie a knot at one end so you can try on your prototype shades and measure the

If the final outcome looks too plain, you can personalize your handmade sunglasses to suit your personality.

cordage around your head. After finding the right length, tie off the other end to the cardboard. Your improvised sunglasses are now done. But you may want to make a fashion statement by using the ballpoint pen to add a little something extra.

SKIN GUARDS

Have you ever heard the saying "an ounce of prevention is worth a pound of cure"? When an emergency happens, it can happen in an instant. You won't always be prepared. This can be especially true concerning the clothes on our back. Clothing helps in maintaining body temperature and protecting us from the

physical environment. In sudden situations we can find ourselves without the proper clothing. I have had to walk through areas with some very irritating and potentially dangerous vegetation. Even wearing proper clothing, certain vegetation still bothered my skin.

There are some natural materials that can be used to create wearable protective barriers. My favorite material to use is tree bark because it is abundant, easy to work with, and tough. Just like unknown food sources, vegetation should be tested on the skin first to avoid any possible reactions. Test a small area of the skin by rubbing it with a sample of the material being used. Wait an hour or two for possible signs of a reaction, such as swelling, reddening of the skin, or itchiness. If anything out of the ordinary appears on the test area, do not use that material.

Patches of green bark can be shaped to fit an area of the body before it dries and hardens, but I prefer to use bark from fallen trees. Place the bark on the area of the body, measure, and cut to fit. Using the reamer or knife, carve out holes on the sides. Cordage can then be threaded through the holes and secured to the body. This simple covering can offer a lot of protection when walking through thick vegetation.

These bark skin guards can be rather robust and give the appearance of a woodland warrior! When securing the guards, take care not to make the cordage too tight around your skin.

HANGER

What You Will Need

- **Small piece of wood with several branches**
- **Wood saw**
- **Knife**
- **Reamer** (optional)
- **Cordage**

ESTIMATED TIME FOR PROJECT

20 minutes

I decided to cut a notch around the piece of wood so that I could hang it by attaching jute twine.

Search the woods high and low for a piece of wood that has several smaller branches coming off of it. Use the wood saw to cut all of the side branches 1 to 2 inches (2.5–5cm) away from the base. Invert the piece of wood so all of the branch bases are pointing upward. There are two options for attaching the cordage in which to hang the hanger from its top: cut a small notch all the way around the branch, or drill a hole with the reamer. Once the cordage is attached, this can be hung from a low-lying branch, or thrown over a high branch in order to raise items off the ground. This is useful for hanging wet clothes, food items, a potholder, and, of course, for hanging your hat up at the end of the day.

SHELF

A shelf will keep items off the ground. Plus, it just makes the campsite a bit cozier. This is a pretty simple project that only requires a bit of cordage, a few pieces of wood, and a wood saw. This shelf won't hold a ton of weight, so the frame doesn't have to be made from very thick-diameter pieces of wood. Of course, the following steps can be adjusted to meet your own specifications.

Use the wood saw to cut equal length pieces of wood that are roughly 1 foot (30cm) long. Next, make a square out of pieces with the ends overlapping each other by a few inches (centimeters). Take the cordage and create lashings around the ends to secure the pieces to one another. Two more lengths of cordage will be used to anchor the shelf to the trunk of the tree. Tie a loop on one end of the cord that can slip over the end of the frame, and wrap the cord around the trunk to the other end of the shelf. Pull the cord taught and tie it off with another loop. Repeat this process for

I used the Hercules model to make this shelf. It's a perfect place to set my cup up off the ground.

the front of the shelf. The cordage for the front needs to be longer because it is going to be wrapped higher up around the trunk. As the frame is leveled out, the cordage will grip the trunk of the tree, allowing the shelf to be suspended. Pieces of bark or several pieces of wood can be used to fill in the platform of the shelf.

NOTCHES

Creating a notch in two opposing pieces of wood will help them to fit together more securely if there is no other means of adhering them together. Whether you are creating a rack for drying meat, making traps, hanging items, or creating a sled, notches can help in building many different types of structures when building materials are tough to come by.

There are two different notches that I have used when crafting out of wood, a straight notch and a dovetail notch. A straight notch is a cut into the wood that resembles half of a rectangle, whereas a dovetail looks like the bottom part of a triangle.

Creating these with the wood saw is very easy. Make the outside notch cuts first to the depth that you need. Then use the saw to cut several straight lines in the wood that is filling the notch. These small sections can be snapped off with the saw or many of the other tools in the Swiss Army Knife. Smooth out the notch by carving out the rough wood with the small blade.

Top: How to start the notch with many cuts that are easy to break out.
Bottom: A dovetail notch.

Campsite

A WORD OF ADVICE

A much more robust version of this could be used to construct a chair low to the ground. Just make sure that the cordage around the tree cannot slip when weight is placed on it.

WOOD PAN HOLDER

In My Experience

When I told my wife I was making a pan holder, I could tell she was holding back laughter. When she saw the finished piece, she said, "That is adorable," to which I replied, "It is a functional accessory to our cookware, thank you very much!"

This holder works well for keeping food warm and off the ground. Place the pan perpendicular to the piece of wood being used so that the right-size notch can be traced. Use the knife to mark indentations in the wood as the outline.

After the initial notch has been cut out, make a slight cut upward for the lip of the pan to sit in.

If you're cooking with this method, make the notch so that the wood frame stays as far away from the fire as possible.

Use the thumb-pushing cutting method (see page 59) to remove most of the wood with the wood saw, which you can also use for the upward cut.

SUSPENDED POT HOLDER

What You Will Need

- **Two to three pieces of wood**
- **Knife**
- **Wood saw**

ESTIMATED TIME FOR PROJECT

15 minutes

At this point you are probably ready to make some dinner. There are some simple frames that can be built with very little physical exertion that will suspend a pot above a fire.

Frame 1

The first frame only requires two pieces of wood and the wood saw. One of the pieces of wood is going to need to have a Y shape in it or a side branch that can be cut off with the wood saw. I suggest that this piece be roughly 4 feet (122cm) long. Measure the piece of wood and use the wood saw to cut it to length.

This suspended pot holder utilizes a frame that may also be constructed with your Swiss Army Knife.

On the end that doesn't have the Y in it, use the knife to create a stake point. A lot of time doesn't need to be spent on the point, since it's only a means of sticking the wood into the ground.

Next, find a much longer piece of wood that will span from the anchor point to over the fire where it will suspend the pot. This piece needs to be green because it needs to bend a bit. Take the piece of wood with the stake point and push it into the ground by the perimeter of the fire. Now place the longer piece of wood onto the other piece of wood so that it is resting in the Y of the branch. The handle of your pot can now slide onto the end of the longer piece of wood and hang over the fire.

Frame 2

The second variation of this pot holder is just as easy to make and only requires a few more piece of wood. Find two branches that are the same length and have a Y shape on the end of them. Sharpen their ends into a point. These two pieces will be the sidebars. Shove one on either side of the fire. A third piece will need to be slightly longer than the width of the two anchor points. This piece will rest horizontally in between the forked branches.

The last piece of construction is a branch to use as a hook for holding the pot handle. If the branch has a hook on the top and bottom, it can be hung as is on the crossbar. If the hook only has one hook, tie it off on a length of cordage to be hung on the crossbar. A little further into the book I discuss how to make a rack for smoking meat (see page 148). If you have already made a frame like that one, you can easily use the cordage method to hang a hook from the top center of the frame.

SLED (TRAVOIS)

The official name for this next project is a travois, although I have also heard it referred to as a drag-along, A-frame, or pull-along. I have always called it a sled, even though it has nothing to do with zooming down a snow-covered hill.

There are times when we cannot carry our packs anymore or need a way to carry extra supplies that we have found, or perhaps need a stretcher to carry others. When this situation arises, constructing a simple sled will help.

The size and length of the pieces of wood used for the sled will be determined by how many supplies you want to carry on it. The pieces of wood used as the sidebars should be roughly 1 inch (2.5cm) in diameter and a minimum of 6 to 8 feet (1.8–2.4m) long. Use the wood saw as the primary cutting tool to quickly gather the materials. Place the tops of the sidebars so that they intersect, forming the top of the letter A. Cut out two notches so that the pieces fit together.

The next piece of wood needs to be several feet (meters) long and will be placed 1 foot (30cm) or so below the notches. This will be used as the handle. Place the handle under the frame and cut notches so that the frame can sit on top of the handle. The handle is used when lifting and pulling the sled. The last few pieces of wood need to be long enough that they span the distance from the bottom of the frame. Fit the pieces together by cutting notches. A minimum of two crossbars should be used, but more can be added depending on how many supplies are being carried. Supplies can now be placed onto the crossbars and tied off with cordage if available. Step into the center of the frame, lift it up by the handle, and start walking!

A WORD OF ADVICE

If you have the cordage to spare, it can be used to secure the pieces together instead of using notches.

Campsite

Food Preparation

One thing I always like using my Swiss Army Knife for is preparing meals. From making cooking utensils or stoves, to offering means to preserve food and physically process food sources, the Swiss Army Knife makes food preparation so much easier.

"Nature does nothing uselessly."
—Aristotle

MAKING TONGS

What You Will Need

- **A piece of wood**
- **Large knife and small knife**
- **Cordage**
- **Larger piece of wood to use as a hammer**

ESTIMATED TIME FOR PROJECT

15 minutes

Just because you're in the wild doesn't mean you have to be uncivilized about everything. Here's how to bring a little bit of convenience and sophistication to food prep by making a simple pair of tongs. Gone are the days of roasting an entire animal leg on a fire spit; now you can cut fillets and brown them evenly by turning them with a pair of tongs.

The size of the tongs required will dictate the size of wood they are made from. Of course, if you choose a branch with a small enough diameter, then you will end up with a pair of chopsticks.

This is a small pair of tongs that I made for my kids to use. Tongs can be used to help cook food as well as grab a hot item.

Food Preparation

METHOD 1

This project will work best with a piece of wood that is as straight as possible. Use the baton method of cutting (page 61) to split the branch down the middle while leaving several inches (centimeters) of solid wood at the bottom.

Tightly wrap the last 1 or 2 inches (2.5–5cm) of the split wood with cordage. This will help keep the wood from splitting all the way apart. Take a thin piece of wood to separate the two halves by pushing it all the way down to where the cordage ends, and trim off the ends. This springs the tongs back open after they have been squeezed shut.

METHOD 2

Another method I have used involves two pieces of wood. Carve one end on each of the sticks at a slight angle so that they fit together better. Begin wrapping the angled ends together with cordage to help hold them in place. Push a small piece of wood in between the two sticks all the way down to the cordage to keep the sticks separated. Finish wrapping cordage around the small piece of wood and the base of the two sticks. The small knife works great for carving the ends of the tongs to the desired shape and size.

USING THE CAN OPENER

What You Will Need

- **Can opener tool**

ESTIMATED TIME FOR PROJECT

1 minute

As with that first Soldier's Knife, most Swiss Army Knives come with a can opener tool. Are we really going to talk about how to open cans? Yes, and for good reason! I would guess that most people have not used what I am going to call an "old-fashioned," manual can opener like those found on the Swiss Army Knife. Fortunately, the can opener is quite easy to use, so don't be frightened. Once you have learned how to use it, you just may prefer it to any other can opener. After the contents of the can have been eaten, be sure to keep the can for the next project!

1. Place the front hook and blade of the can opener on the inside top of the can. The initial cut can be the hardest. Sometime I will tap the top of the can opener to help push the tip into the metal.

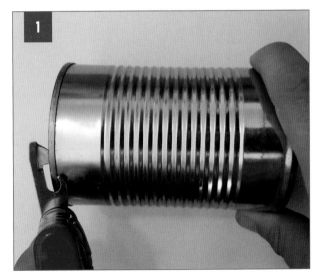

2. Place the back hook on the underside of the can lip. As you raise the opener up and down, rotate the can with your other hand until the can lid has been cut all the way around.

If the lid happens to make that harrowing dive and falls into the food, just use the tip of the can opener to fish it out.

The can opener isn't just for opening tins, though. There are also a few other food-related tasks that I have used the can opener for. My favorite type of nut is the pistachio, but sometimes they are tough to open. One of the more sophisticated ways I have used the can opener is to pry open those tough shells. It also works very well as a fruit peeler—I have taken off many orange skins with this little guy. I even used it once as a small gut hook.

ALUMINUM STOVE (HOBO STOVE)

What You Will Need

- **Soup or coffee can that is metal**
- **Wire or nails for the grill** (optional)
- **Reamer/punch tool**
- **Scissors**
- **Pliers**

ESTIMATED TIME FOR PROJECT

20–30 minutes

Hobo stoves were generally large metal drums that were turned upside down in order to have a cooking surface. They can also be used to warm up people huddled around them. In the survivalist community, hobo stoves tend to be made from smaller containers to create a small, portable cooking/heating source. I have used coffee, soup, and soda cans.

Knowing how to make these simple stoves is a great skill to have. They are easily transported once made. And the materials needed to make one are found everywhere, as they are thrown out as trash, so these stoves cost almost nothing to make.

As they are, the cans can obviously contain a fire, but they lack the proper airflow to keep a good fire going. Using the punch to create holes in the can will allow air in to feed the fire. Even just a few holes along the perimeter of the bottom of the can will make a huge difference. Do not use the reamer, as its blade may be damaged. Soda cans will be easier to puncture than the thicker walls of coffee and soup cans.

1. Make an opening at the bottom of the can to feed fuel through after the fire has been started. This will keep you from having to constantly remove your cup or cooking dish in order to drop wood in. The metal saw can be used, but it makes the work a bit tedious. Surprisingly, the scissors can cut through the walls of a soup can with ease. Use a few holes that were made from the bottom of the can as the starting point for the scissors. This will be where the fuel is inserted later.

Food Preparation

2. If you feel like going the extra mile, a grill attachment can be added so that whatever is placed on top doesn't suffocate the fire as much. It also gives you a place to roast small pieces of meat. Puncture six to eight holes: three to four on each opposing side of the can near the top. Insert a couple of nails or any other small-diameter pieces of metal that will be strong enough to act as a grill top. (I used some lengths of copper that I found lying around.) The wires need to be tight so that they don't sag when weight is placed on top. I used the pliers on my SwissChamp to pull and bend the ends of the copper around the lip of the can.

3. I initially placed burning material in through the top and started the fire through the bottom opening. With a smaller opening at the bottom of the can, the fire tends to burn hotter. Since the fire is contained in a small area, it will burn quickly. Fuel will need to be fed into the can frequently.

4. This hobo stove boiled a half cup of water in ten minutes. The raised grill allows the flames to come out of the top and surround the cup. As you can see, with the cup on top, there isn't much room to add wood. That opening at the bottom comes in handy.

A WORD OF ADVICE

Coming across copper, nails, or other lengths of wire may be a rare find, so here is another option for making the top of the stove. Use the metal saw to cut four notches out around the perimeter of the top. This will allow for cookware to be placed on top without suffocating the fire.

Here is a second option for the hobo stove if you don't want to include the grill attachment but still want a cooking surface. For this method, the can will be flipped over so that the bottom is now the top and will be the cooking surface. Holes will need to be punctured around the top and bottom for airflow and venting purposes, and fuel for the fire will need to be fed through a small section cut out of the can. Since the fire will now be sitting on the ground, the can will need to be placed in a dry location. I used an aluminum coffee can in this demonstration.

1. After tracing an outline on the bottom of the can, use the reamer tool to cut several holes. The metal saw or scissors can be used to cut along the dotted line. The metal saw must be used in order to cut through the thicker rim at the bottom. The reamer/punch was used to punch several holes around the perimeter of the bottom, as well as to make a vent on the side near the top of the can.

2. It's easier to place the can over a small fire that has already been started rather than try to start one inside the can.

3. Once the can is in place, fuel will be fed in through the bottom opening.

4. Use a fork (like the one I whittled previously, page 67) to make sure the meat browns evenly.

SODA CAN ALCOHOL STOVE

What You Will Need

- **Two aluminum soda cans**
- **Can opener tool**
- **Knife blade**
- **Scissors**
- **Alcohol or other flammable liquid** (70% IPA seems to work best)

ESTIMATED TIME FOR PROJECT

20–30 minutes

There are different variations of this stove, but I'm going to show you the simplest one that I always make. I really like these types of projects because the materials can be found almost anywhere, even out in the wilderness. An added bonus for this type of stove is how compact it is. This one can fit in your pocket!

Having a Swiss Army Knife model with a can opener tool, knife, and scissors will make this project much easier. A quick word of warning: just like the hobo stove project, these cans are going to have extremely sharp edges as they are cut apart. Take your time and be careful!

1. Find two soda cans and cut out the concave bottom of one of the cans. The aluminum is thicker on this part of the can, but the can opener can make this step easier. Hold the can opener almost parallel to the can and apply more pressure to the front cutting tip rather than the back curved lip of the opener. As you get to the end of the cut, be careful not to put too much pressure on the can or the lip will start to bend.

2. Now you need to decide how big or small you want your stove to be. The smaller the stove is, the more durable it will be and the longer it will last bouncing around inside a pack. Mine ended up being about the thickness of my SwissChamp. The way I did this was to extend the small blade and place the SwissChamp on a flat surface. Next, situate the knife so that the tip or the blade is touching the can. With one hand holding the SwissChamp and one hand holding the can, rotate the can several times against the small blade. This will produce a score mark that will go all the way around the can. Keep the whole knife as flat as possible when making the score mark.

3. Puncture a small hole along the score line with the knife blade. A hole large enough for the scissors to be inserted is all you need.

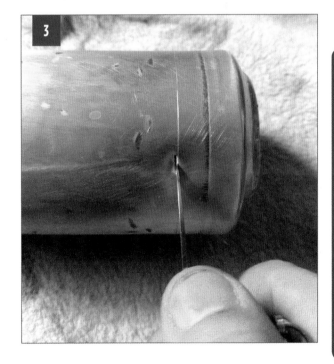

4. From this starting point, use the scissors to easily cut along the line. I always err on the waste side of the cut. More can always be cut off later. Positioning the scissors at a slight downward angle, so that the points are going into the can, helps to prevent the scissors from binding between the metal. This piece will be the top of the stove. Take the other can and repeat the scoring and cutting steps above. DO NOT repeat the can opener step, as we need the bottom intact.

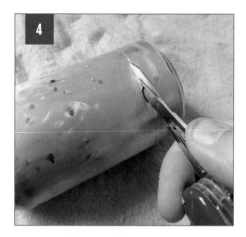

5. There should now be two bottom pieces that were cut from the cans. One will have a hole in it and the other will have a solid bottom. The piece with the solid bottom is the bottom of the stove. All of the dimples along the lip of the top of the stove are where the can opener began to crimp the metal a bit. At this point the stove just needs to be put together and it will be done.

6. Carefully slide the two pieces into one another so that the can with the hole in it is at one end and the bottom piece is at the other end. The top should be on the inside of the bottom can. This part can be a bit tricky. I find that working slowly and not applying too much pressure at first really helps to not crimp the metal. Work from one end and rotate the pieces while gently pressing the top into the bottom. Be extra careful on this step, because the edges are very sharp.

7. Once the top is about halfway inserted, use the palm of your hand to press the top all the way into the bottom. Any remaining sharp edges can be cut off with the scissors and rounded with the metal file.

8. Now all that is left is to add the fuel. Any flammable liquid will work in this stove, but I have found that 70% IPA (isopropyl alcohol), or rubbing alcohol, works very well. Unlike burning wood, an alcohol stove burns very clean, producing almost no smoke. I used a capful of lighter fluid here just to show that other liquids can be used in this stove.

This kind of stove can be used for a heat source to warm up on a cold night or for cooking purposes. You'll need to construct a way to suspend your cookware above the stove, as this type of stove doesn't really allow for a pot or pan to be placed on it.

Food Preparation

KABOB SKEWER

Whether it be a minnow or even an insect, it will most likely go down easier if cooked. Because of its small nature, it may be hard to figure out how to cook it, especially if gear is in limited supply. But small detail work is where the Swiss Army Knife really shines.

It would be hard to make thin kabobs with a larger knife, as it would most likely break the wood. The thin profile of the Swiss Army Knife makes it much easier to create thin pieces of wood. These thin pieces of wood are ideal for roasting small food over a fire. Taper one end of a piece of wood into a spear point. Use the small knife to profile the rest of the wood into a smaller diameter.

Use the pliers to grab handles or the lip of a container.

USING THE HOOK TOOL

It is easy to leave cookware on the fire too long and then it becomes hotter than you expect. You probably didn't pack those awesome potholders that our grandmas crocheted, so we need another way to get those hot items off the fire.

I have used two sticks as an improvised pair of tongs (see page 133), but I tend to spill a lot. Instead, try using the pliers for holding onto that hot cup or small cooking container when removing it from the heat source. If you are using a pot or kettle that has a wire handle, the hook tool will be your next best friend.

This is one of my favorite uses for the hook tool.

WHO KNEW? THE MANY USES OF THE HOOK

In my life I have run into a few people who own a Swiss Army Knife but are not using it to its full potential. During the process of comparing our knives, inevitably the other person extends the hook tool and says, "What the heck am I ever going to use this for?" Surprisingly, the hook tool is quite useful if one takes the time to think about it.

With the hook tool extended, wrap up the frame of the knife with cordage. This can now be used as an improvised grappling hook, or lowered to retrieve fallen items.

It can be used to help carry items in a few different ways. Use the hook to hold onto a strap while using the frame of the Swiss Army Knife as a handle to hold onto. I have also used the hook to help carry firewood. Simply tie cordage around the firewood and hook onto the cordage.

If you are carrying or pulling a load that has been tied up with cordage, don't hurt your hands by pulling the cordage. Instead, hook onto the cordage and use the Swiss Army Knife as a handle.

The hook can be inserted into the mouth or gills of a slippery fish.

Is there a tight space you are trying to push cordage through? Insert the hook and grab onto the end of the cordage and pull it through.

The hook can help to free a stuck zipper.

I have even used the hook as an improvised shoehorn.

I have trouble with those "easy-to-open" soup cans with the pull-tab on them. Somehow, I always end up breaking the tab off! I'll use the can opener to pry the tab up and then the hook to pull on it.

It's probably hard to tell from my author photo, but I am a little on the short side and have trouble reaching stuff sometimes. The hook gives me that much-needed little bit of reach to grab onto something.

If you need some sophistication in the wild, hang the Swiss Army Knife from a limb by the key ring and use the hook to hang your hat on after a long day!

Threading cordage through the key ring twice will keep the cordage from slipping. It also gives a secondary anchor point so you don't lose your Swiss Army Knife.

Instead of trying to hold a bunch of wood in your arms, wrap it up in cordage and use the hook to carry the load.

Food Preparation

SMOKING MEAT

Wouldn't it be nice to save some food for later? Smoking is an easy way to preserve meat so that you can do so. Dehydrating meat helps prevent the growth of any organisms, and the smoke creates an outer protective layer, almost like a varnish. There are essentially two methods for smoking: hot smoking and cold smoking. Hot smoking uses heat and smoke to cook the meat. It usually involves creating a structure around the fire in which to trap the heat and the smoke. Cold smoking is done more in the open, at low temperatures, with the smoke passing over the meat. The smoking process can take a long time, but it will allow the meat to be carried safely for a few extra days.

A very simple drying rack can be constructed with minimal supplies. Take two sidebars and create spear points at one end so that they can be secured into the ground. If cordage is unavailable, choose pieces of wood that have several smaller branch offshoots, or else cut notches into the sidebars with the saw and knife. This is where the crossbeams will sit.

Place one of the sidebars on each side of the fire, but not close enough that the wood will burn. Next, choose smaller branches for the crossbars, which should be small enough to fit into the notches, long enough to span the sidebars, and sturdy enough to support the weight of the meat. Attach the crossbars and hang the meat.

The idea is that the smoke is "cooking" the meat more than the actual heat of the fire, so don't hang the meat too close to the flames. When it comes to anything that I am consuming, I always like to err on the side of safety. For this reason I would continue the smoking process until the meat is almost hard or brittle. Think of jerky.

A single shelf or several can be made depending on how much meat needs to be smoked. Strips of meat should be placed over the wood so that they are hanging. By adding a few more sticks, I made a shelf where I can keep my cup of coffee warm.

Food Preparation

Fishing

Fishing is a long-standing means of obtaining food in the wild, but it is not as easy as some like to believe. I find it interesting that, although our fishing gear has become more advanced, how we catch fish has remained the same: with traps, nets, spears, or hook and bait.

A WORD OF ADVICE

The corkscrew tool can act as a fishing line holder. I can get roughly 25 feet (7.6m) of fishing line with a hook tied around the corkscrew and still have it open and close properly. The line can get a bit tangled when you go to use it, but it will straighten itself out. Tie the end of the line at the base of the corkscrew so you can hold onto the frame of the knife while throwing out your hook. Make sure to hold on tight in case you hook a big one—you don't want to lose your Swiss Army Knife fishing pole!

The model size of your Swiss Army Knife will dictate how much fishing line you can add. A small rock sinker can be added later in the field.

Of course, there are a few other primitive fishing methods that are not as well known. There are many indigenous cultures that implement a poisoning method, using plants, barks, seeds, and fruits that are toxic to fish. Mashed up, these release chemical toxins. When placed in a body of water, the toxins pass over the fish's gills and the fish becomes stunned, floating to the surface where it may easily be collected.

I cannot say this for a fact, but throwing rocks and sticks at the water was probably the very first way in which a fish was caught—I don't see how it can get more basic than that. The obvious intention is to strike a fish directly, but that is actually not necessary in order for this method to work. Think of a time when you were in a swimming pool and under the surface of the water. What happens when someone jumps in the water close by or hits the surface of the water with his or her hand? It creates a shockwave that we can physically feel. Since fish are much more sensitive to this kind of physical stimulation, you can use that to your advantage. By taking a large branch and striking the water as hard as possible near a fish, it can create enough of a shockwave that will stun the fish, causing it to float to the surface.

Here are some tips to keep in mind when fishing. **Small fish** are more abundant in the shallows along the water's edge. I have also found that they tend to be less skittish to my presence. I can lean over the water's edge and small fish will still swim up to a hook to investigate. If I try to walk up to a **large fish,** it will usually swim away. When trying to catch larger fish, it is best to stand away from the edge of the water, especially if the sun is behind you. A shadow cast onto the water will scare fish away. A good place to try and catch fish is around structures in the water where they can hide, such as a downed tree, or under rocks.

> *"Nature is cheaper than therapy."*
> **—M.P. Zarrella**

A WORD OF ADVICE

Check your local regulations regarding permissible fishing methods.

Even fishing offers opportunities to use your Swiss Army Knife.

When possible, use bait that is natural to the area, because that is what the fish are used to eating. Watching the surface of the water can give clues as to what the fish are eating.

If you are fishing with a hook and line, don't be discouraged if you can't find any bait. Sometimes, perhaps out of curiosity, a fish will mouth a hook with no bait. It may be a little difficult, but by throwing line and hook over a fish, you can hook it in the body. I have only hooked a fish in this manner by accident, and it is against some local laws; however, if you find yourself in a survival situation, it is another means of catching food.

Now that you have some basic information about fishing, let's see what the Swiss Army Knife can do to increase your chances of having fish for dinner.

In My Experience

One day when I was out fishing, I ran out of worms to use for bait. I didn't feel like calling it a day, so I sat there by the water enjoying the nice weather. I started to hear this "plopping" sound. A little way downstream was a tree with branches overhanging the water. Every so often a small berry would drop from one of the branches and float on top of the water. It didn't take long for a fish to come up and grab it. I took a few of those berries, placed one on a small hook, and threw it into the water next to where they were falling from the tree. Almost instantly a small fish swam up and swallowed the bait. That was probably the quickest I had ever caught a fish.

PARACORD FISHING NET

Sometimes I see a stick and think, "Hmm, what can I make out of that?" That is exactly what happened when I found this little gem lying in the grass. I thought the natural Y shape of the stick would be a good frame for a paracord fishing net. Here's how to make a quick fishing net using a simple overhand knot.

If this branch had been thicker, it could have made a really big slingshot.

1. Smooth out the frame by removing the bark with the small knife. Use the wood saw to remove any spots where smaller branches had grown out. It's not necessary to remove the bark; I merely did so for aesthetic reasons. Next I prepared the cordage I was going to use. You can use whatever is available to you, such as jute twine, string, rope, or paracord. I chose paracord because it is so widely used and very strong. This fishing net is not going to be very big, so the length of the paracord I used was cut into roughly 5 foot (1.5m)-long sections. After the length is cut, take one end and match it up with the other end so that the cordage is doubled over and creates a loop on one end. Place the looped end behind the frame. If you place this kind of loop close to the end, cut a notch into the wood so that the loop doesn't slip off the end.

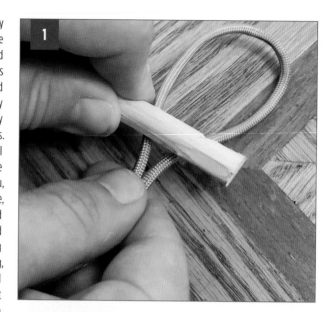

2. Pull the loop over the frame toward your body. Make sure to keep the ends of the cord even.

3. Pull the two pieces of cordage up and all the way through the loop. It helps to keep one finger on top of the wood and to reach into the loop with your other finger and pull the cords through.

4. Pull the two pieces of cordage until the loop is tightened. As you pull the cord taught, you may need to pull backward a bit to cinch the loop around the wood.

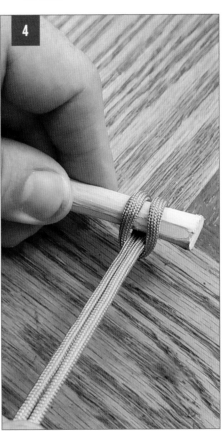

Fishing

5. The space between the knots in the net depends on how close or far apart the starting loops are from one another. The size of the net will determine how many of these lines you start off with. For this net, I started off with six of these individual lines. I chose two different colors of paracord to make it easier to see.

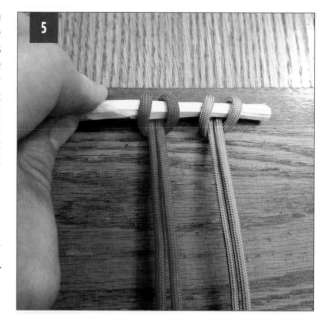

6. Take two of the inner individual cords, pull taught, and tie in an overhand knot. To do this, wrap the two cords around your fingers to make a single loop. Keep the cord that is coming from the previous knot as straight as possible.

7. Pull the ends of the two cords through the loop from behind. When using two different colors, it helps to keep the colors on consistent sides after each knot.

8. Repeat this process all the way around, and that is how you make the net pattern. The lines will crisscross back and forth as you move down the lines. You will know that you are doing the pattern correctly if you are making the diamond and triangle shapes as you progress.

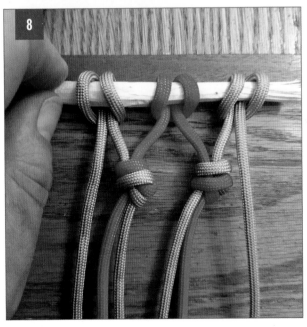

9. The colors don't have to be consistent for the net pattern to still function correctly. When done correctly, the cords will make a zigzag pattern from each knot.

10. When making a net in a circle, the net will get smaller and smaller as you move your way down the lines. A round net will start to look like a basketball hoop's net toward the bottom.

11. When you get to the point where there is only enough cordage left to make one knot, make that knot as close to the previous one as possible. Use the scissors to cut the excess cordage from the knot ends, and burn the ends with a lighter to prevent fraying. While the bottom of the net is much smaller than the top, it is still open. Thread a small length of extra cordage in and out between the cordage just above the last knots in the net. Double this over the end, pull tight, and finish with two overhand knots. After the excess cord has been cut, the burned ends should look similar to this.

A WORD OF ADVICE

When removing large amounts of wood shavings and bark from these projects, keep the shavings! They are easily carried and can be used as tinder for fire starting.

This is the amount of tinder I collected from the fishing net project.

Fishing

Use Excess Paracord to Wrap the Handle

There are so many different and beautiful patterns that people use for handles. I have a go-to method that is quick and easy.

Measure the length you want your handle. Place one end of your cordage at the base and make a loop the length of the handle. Starting at the bottom, take the longer end of the cordage and begin wrapping upward. When you get close to the top, thread the end of the cord you were wrapping with through the loop at the top. Grab the end of the cord at the bottom of the handle and pull (pliers may be needed). This will close the loop at the top, pulling the cordage tight and a bit under the handle. Use the scissors to cut the excess cordage and burn with a lighter.

I found a nice place to hang the net up at the end of the day.

KEY RING FISHING HOOK

What You Will Need

- **Key ring from the Swiss Army Knife**
- **Can opener tool**
- **Metal file**

ESTIMATED TIME FOR PROJECT

15 minutes

About to sacrifice a piece off this Swiss Army Knife.

Believe it or not, you can remove the key ring to fashion a small hook for fishing. It takes a little effort, but it really works! I used the key ring from one of my Tinker models to make the hook. The first time I used this technique was about twenty years ago. I discovered it not through a survival situation but out of boredom.

When it comes to fishing, I am generally a catch-and-release person, and on one particular day I was catching fish left and right. It may sound odd, but it got to the point where I was catching so many fish that it became predictable and boring. I stopped fishing for a bit and whittled away at a piece of wood. The key ring on the knife was clanging away against the frame as I did so, forcing me to notice it. I wondered what interesting thing I could do with it. The following project is the result.

1. Remove the key ring from the frame of the knife. To do this, slightly bend one of the end prongs of the ring away from the main body of the ring. Then, simply turn the ring like you would when adding or removing keys to a key ring. Do this until it is separated from the frame. If you are having trouble getting a fingernail to pry the key ring open, try using the tweezers.

2. Next, create the shape of the hook. Use the can opener; its shape and different angles allow it to get into the tight spaces of the key ring. Simply slide the blade side between the two pieces of metal that make up the ring and pry the metal apart by using your thumb or finger to hold the piece of the ring that is already bent outward. Then push the ring in the opposite direction.

3. As you begin to pry the single piece of metal apart, maintain the integrity of the ring. This will be the anchor point in which the fishing line or cordage will be attached.

4. Use a hard surface, such as a rock, along with the can opener tool to help bend the metal into the hook shape you want. Take care not to twist the metal too much, so you don't break the ring in half. If broken, the ring can still be fashioned into a hook, but it is much harder to do so. After the shape has been created, use the metal file or a rock to help sharpen the point of the hook.

Now all that is left is to attach your line. Fishing line, the inner strands of paracord, or anything else handy should be threaded into the ring portion and tied off with a knot. It takes some practice to get a feel for the hook, but I have caught a few fish with this.

WOOD FISHING HOOKS

Wood and bone fishing hooks have been used throughout history as a way to catch fish. The key ring fishing hook set me on a path to using "primitive" hooks in order to see what I could catch. Those around me have often given me odd looks upon seeing what I was using for tackle. Those looks quickly turned to nods of approval when I would catch more fish than them sometimes!

Just because a tool or technique is considered primitive doesn't mean that it is no longer effective—it can sometimes be even better than what we use today. Carving the hook out of a single, straight piece of wood will make it stronger, but this will require a bit more time. It will go quicker if you find a smaller piece of wood that is forked. The size of the hook is going to depend on the size of fish available that you are trying to catch. A large hook will allow you to only catch large fish, whereas a small hook will allow you to catch large and small fish.

1. Finding a branch that is forked will make it quicker to fashion the hook portion.
2. Use the small blade to carve one side into a spear point for the hook.
3. Don't cut too much off below the V. If that section becomes too thin, the hook will easily snap.
4. With the knife, carve a notch all the way around the top shaft of the hook. This will make it easier when tying off the cordage.
5. Use a piece of fishing line or other cordage to tie off the hook.

Carving small, wood hooks can be delicate work, so use light fingers.

GORGE HOOKS

What You Will Need

- **A small piece of strong wood, animal bone, horn, or thorns**
- **Cordage and bait**
- **Wood saw and knife**

ESTIMATED TIME FOR PROJECT

15 minutes

A gorge is a very basic type of hook, sharpened on both ends so it becomes lodged inside the fish when swallowed. The size of the gorge is going to be determined by the size of the fish you are trying to catch. I suggest starting out making one that is 1 inch (2.5cm) long. Measure a piece of wood and, using the knife, sharpen both ends to a spear point. Cut a shallow groove in the center of the gorge that goes all the way around the hook. This groove is going to be where the fishing line ties onto the hook.

When baiting the hook, it is very important that the bait and hook line up parallel to the fishing line. This helps so that even a small fish can swallow it. It ensures that the gorge travels further down past the mouth to where it can be more effective. When actively fishing, give plenty of slack when a fish has taken the bait. Time and slack

are needed so that the fish swallows the bait before pulling on the line. When the line is sharply tugged, it will pull the gorge from the middle and turn it sideways, lodging itself inside the fish.

Be careful not to make the middle or the side points too thin, or it could break when attempting to set the hook.

A WORD OF ADVICE

Be sure to check regulations in your area to ensure that the fishing methods you intend to practice are allowed.

Fishing

METAL FISHING HOOKS

What You Will Need

- **Metal tab**
- **Metal saw or file**
- **Cordage**

ESTIMATED TIME FOR PROJECT

10 minutes

If you happen upon an old soda can or soup can, a fishing hook can be made from its pull tab. It is not the sturdiest of hooks, but it will work in a pinch. If you fish from the shore like I usually do, you probably don't carry a large tackle box with you.

Make your own metal fishing hook:

1. Remove the pull tab from a can.
2. Use the metal saw to cut through the larger "loop" in the tab.
3. Use the metal file to sharpen and shape the point of the hook.
4. Use cordage to tie off the smaller loop of the tab, and you are ready to fish!

In My Experience

Fishing can be a frustrating activity. One day my line kept breaking, my bait was being taken, the tip of my fishing pole snapped, and I had to stop because I lost all of my hooks. I threw my hands up and began walking back to my vehicle.

Along the way, I came upon a littered area where people had recently camped. I took a few minutes to collect the cans and bottles that had been scattered on the ground. Maybe it was because I had hooks on my mind, but I noticed how the pull tab on the cans resembled the shape and size of a fishing hook. Right then and there I created my first metal fishing hook and tried it out. While I was able to hook some fish in the mouth, doing so was difficult and increased the likelihood of bending the soft metal. This is why when I use these I allow the fish to swallow the hook before trying to pull it in.

Pictured left to right: Soda can tab fishing hook, key ring fishing hook, and two different styles of wood fishing hooks. The blackened paracord on the far right hook is where I melted the cordage with a lighter. This helps to adhere the pieces together and creates a nice bond.

SPRING FISHING HOOKS

The scissor spring can easily be turned into a fishing hook. One end of the spring is already curled into a nice eye where the cordage can be threaded.

I used the pliers to pull and bend the spring backward 180°. All that was left was to thread some inner strand of paracord through the eye and tie it off.

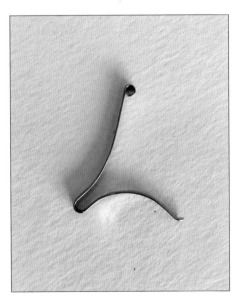

Here is the spring after I removed it from the scissors.

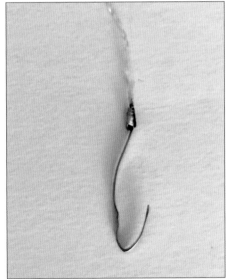

Here is the finished hook. Since there is still a bit of spring to this hook's step, it would work best for small fish or fish with "soft" mouths. When using this hook, you need to have a gentle touch when reeling the fish in.

WAYS TO USE THE FISHING HOOKS

I think we tend to get stuck on one method of fishing with hooks—a fishing pole—but there are other methods. Now that we know how to make a variety of fishing hooks, let's look at some ways that they can be used.

Handline fishing is just what it sounds likes: you hold the fishing line in your hands as you cast and reel in the line. It requires the least amount of gear to carry, which is nice if you're on a long hike. But it can be a little rough on the hands, especially when trying to pull in larger fish, so wrap the line around a smooth rock or a small piece of wood as you reel it in.

In My Experience

When my mom was little, she went fishing with her dad quite often, and they mainly used cane poles. Cane poles are usually made from cane, but my mom told me that they would make them out of saplings or a long branch. I thought she was pulling my leg, so the next time we went fishing she made me leave my pole in the car. We found a branch lying on the ground that was about 6 feet (1.8m) long. She showed me how to wrap the line around the pole all the way to the tip where it was tied off, leaving about 10 to 15 feet (3–4.5m) of line hanging off. Before I knew it, I was pulling in bluegills and sunfish left and right. Thanks, Mom, for showing me how to catch fish with a stick.

"Active fishing" requires a person to physically be present while fishing, but in a survival situation you may not have the time to stand around all day trying to catch a fish. The following are a few ways to leave hooks out so that other tasks can be accomplished. I call the following method **"line fishing,"** and it requires a bit more cordage and several hooks.

- Tie off individual lines and hooks at intervals along a long length of cordage so that they are hanging down.
- Take the main line of cordage and secure it between two objects, such as two trees, so that the line is strung across the top of the water. Having several hooks in the water will increase the chances of catching a fish.

A WORD OF ADVICE

If you are having difficultly removing a hook from a fish, use the hook disgorger and press the hook into the fish slightly in order to take pressure off the barb.

When not fishing to sustain yourself, fish may be released after being caught.

If you are unable to string the line across the water, the line can be used in a slightly different way:

- Anchor one end of the line on the shore and tie the other end of the line to a heavy rock.
- Throw the rock out and into the water so that the mainline is stretched out.

A benefit of this method is that it allows you to expand your dinner menu. Fishing at different depths allows for different kinds of fish to be caught.

Jug fishing is basically fishing with a very large bobber! This utilizes a plastic bottle with a cap—a 2-liter bottle works best.

- Tie off a line and hook around the neck of the bottle, just below the cap.
- In this same spot, tie off another line to retrieve the bottle.
- Throw the bottle and hook into the water, and be sure to tightly tie off the retrieving line on shore.

This can be set and forgotten, allowing you to attend to other tasks. When a fish has taken the bait, the bottle will bob up and down to indicate that it has been hooked. Pull in the retrieving line and see what you caught!

FISHING BOBBER

What You Will Need

- **A piece of wood**
- **Cordage**
- **Reamer** (but the tip of the knife will work in a pinch)

ESTIMATED TIME FOR PROJECT

15 minutes

Using a larger piece of wood in this fashion allows it to be used for a variety of other functions, such as a handle, a toggle, or a way to keep two lines of cordage separated.

Using a bobber is how a person should learn how to fish first because it lets you know when a fish first starts to show interest in the bait. A simple piece of wood can be used as a fishing bobber since wood floats. I have tried various ways of tying cordage to a wood bobber, but I have found that the best way to attach it is by drilling two holes into the wood.

- Drill two holes into the wood with the reamer, and thread the cordage through them; this makes the bobber easily adjustable and ensures that the bobber will not detach from the fishing line. Having an adjustable bobber will allow you to fish at different depths.
- Tie a small rock around the line for a sinker.

If the end of the fishing line is properly weighted, a fishing bobber such as this should stand upright in the water, making it easily visible.

PARACORD FISHING FLY

What You Will Need

- **Small piece of paracord**
- **A hook**
- **Knife blade or scissors**
- **Cordage**
- **Lighter**

ESTIMATED TIME FOR PROJECT

10 minutes

It may seem silly to think that you can catch a fish using a piece of cordage as bait, but I have even caught fish with nothing on my hook. Paracord fishing flies are incredibly easy to make and surprisingly effective at grabbing that stubborn fish's attention. You will need a bit of paracord (a bright color works best), a fishing hook, a flame, and of course your Swiss Army Knife.

1. Cut the paracord so that the end is open, exposing the inner strands.

2. Use the knife or scissors to cut into and fray all of the ends as much as possible. Rub the frays vigorously against your hand to fluff them up.

3. Make a cut approximately ¼ inch (6mm) from the end (you can make the fly whatever size you desire).

4. Melt the end that has not been frayed. This step can also be done after you have inserted the hook. Melting the nylon around the hook helps the fly from accidently falling off. This step is optional but recommended.

5. Throw your line out a number of times consecutively in the same spot before letting it stay in the water.

I like to wrap more of the white inner paracord strand around the body of the fly because it gives it a little more weight and color.

Fishing

JUG FISH TRAP

What You Will Need

- **2-liter plastic bottle**
- **Knife or scissors**
- **Cordage**

ESTIMATED TIME FOR PROJECT

5-10 minutes

You will notice throughout this book that some of the materials I am using would be considered trash by most people. Not me! I love to repurpose material as much as I can, especially from trash because it can be found everywhere. This project will help to catch small to medium fish that can be eaten or used as bait for larger fish.

- Cut a 2-liter soda bottle just below the neck, then invert the top so that the neck of the bottle is now sticking into the body of the bottle.
- Place a piece of bait (insects, worms, or rancid meat will work) that will sit in the bottom and lure the fish into the trap.

- Place the trap along the edge of a body of water where smaller fish spend most of their time. The idea here is that, when submerged in water, fish will swim into the bottle to eat the bait but then will not be able to get back out.

The original opening is quite small and will allow minnows and small prey to enter the trap. The top can be cut to create a larger opening in hopes of catching bigger fish. I like to puncture four small holes (two anchor points at minimum) along the cut line in order to tie the two pieces of plastic together. It doesn't always happen, but if the inverted top is not sewn into the bottle, it can be pushed out, allowing your catch to escape. If you're in dire circumstances, you don't want to take any chances with losing a possible meal, no matter how small it is.

A WORD OF ADVICE

Be sure to check regulations in your area to ensure that the fishing methods you intend to practice are allowed.

Be sure to anchor or place the jug in such a way that it doesn't float or drift away. This could also be used as a collection container when foraging for wild edibles.

In My Experience

I was looking for a good spot to fish from when suddenly I saw a man sitting on a bucket in front of me. He showed me his homemade jug fish trap and told me how he used it to catch small baitfish. He then showed me that the bucket he was sitting on was full of larger fish that he had caught using the baitfish. Ever since then, I have always used as much natural bait as possible from the surrounding area in which I am fishing.

FISHING STRINGER

What You Will Need

- **Cordage**
- **Knife**
- **Reamer**

ESTIMATED TIME FOR PROJECT

20 minutes

A fish stringer is a piece of cordage with a loop on one end and needlelike tip on the other. It can be used to keep fish alive in the water after being caught or for carrying multiple fish at once.

- Find a piece of wood that is at least the thickness of a pencil and about 6 inches (15cm) long. The length of the wood is not that critical, as you will see. I will be referring to the piece of wood as the "needle" because that is what it resembles.

- On one end, use the reamer to carve out a hole in the wood that goes all the way through. This area of the wood needs to be strong, so if it starts to split, get a slightly thicker piece of wood. With the reamer or knife, slightly round off the edge of the hole to make it less abrasive against the cordage.

- Use the small knife to create a spear point on the opposite end of the hole.

- Smooth out any other sections as needed along the needle, but don't remove too much wood.

- Thread the cordage through the hole and secure it to the needle with your choice of knot.

- Make a loop on the opposite end of the cordage. Be sure that your knots are strong so that the fish don't get away! The stringer is now done, so let's talk for a moment about how to use this overly simple thing.

You have just caught a fish but you want to keep it alive for awhile because you are not ready to go back to camp. The stringer needs to be used in order to hold onto the fish, so that it can be placed back into the water and kept alive. There are two ways in which I have used a stringer; the first way I'm going to call the "old school" way because it was the way I was first taught.

Thread the needle into the fish's mouth and out through the gills. Then, take the needle and thread it through the small loop at the end of the cordage. A larger loop has just been made that can be tightened all the way down to the fish. Anchor the needle end of the cordage by pushing it firmly into the ground, laying a heavy rock on it or tying it off to some object. The fish can now be put back into the water to keep it alive without the worry of it swimming away. As more fish are caught, simply thread the needle through the gills and slide each one down to the fish already on the line.

I do not use this method as much anymore because sometimes it can kill the fish. It wouldn't always happen, but I found that I would end up with one or several fish on my stringer that would die even though they were back in the water. Fish use their gills in order to breathe underwater, so you can think of the gills as "lungs." The stringer can interfere with this process and cause death.

I like to double up my cordage so that I can make the stringer longer if I need to.

A friend showed me a different way to use the stringer, and I don't think I have had a fish die on me yet with this alternate method. The process is essentially the same as above, except the stringer does not go through the gills. Instead, open the fish's mouth and push the needle through the soft tissue on the bottom of the mouth. In this way, the loop is made around the fish's lip and not its gills.

Fishing

Collecting and Cleaning Water

Water is essential to life. Following the aforementioned rule of threes (page 72), a person can survive three days without water. There are documented cases of people living much longer than three days without water, but I do not recommend pushing the limit. By day three, without water you will most likely be experiencing severe headaches, dizziness, joint and muscle ache, lack of energy, and hallucinations. At this point, though still alive, the situation will only continue to deteriorate due to lack of productiveness. You may find yourself away from a major water source like a pond, lake, stream, or river, but there are other means in which to obtain water. Knowing how to do so is a critical skill.

When looking for water, always travel downhill. Small pools of water can be collected in low points. Look under rocks, in holes in the ground, and in heavily shaded areas. Just because we can't see the water doesn't mean it's not there. If there is enough ground water, a small well can be created by digging a hole into the earth. After some time, water will begin to seep into the hole, leaving a small pool. Following a dry river or stream bed may lead to a spot where water has collected in low points, or just beneath the ground as well. Let's take a look at a few more options for collecting and cleaning water in our surroundings.

Collecting from Vegetation

There are a number of ways to collect water directly from vegetation. They work best if you have access to a piece of plastic, which is why it is a good idea to always have a few trash bags in your survival kit.

Wrap a piece of plastic around several **branches of a tree** that have a lot of green leaves. Use cordage to tie off the end of the

There are times when water is right in front of us but for some reason it may be difficult to collect. I was once on a hike with an old-timer when he stopped us by a rock face. There was a little stream of water flowing out of the rock, traveling down several feet, and then disappearing back into the rock. Looking over at me, he asked that I collect some of the water into my water bottle. Naturally, I removed the lid and pressed the lip of the water bottle onto the rock face. The flow of the water was so low that it simply went around the top of the bottle and continued its way down the rock. Finally I looked at him and shrugged. He smiled a bit, bent down, and began to unlace one of his bootlaces. With the tip of his knife, he was able to press part of the bootlace into a tiny crack that was under the stream of water. He then placed the rest of the bootlace into my water bottle and told me to back up slightly so that the bootlace was pulled away from the wall. After some time, a drop of water appeared at the end of the lace and dropped into the bottle. The drips of water steadily increased in frequency and began to slowly fill the bottle up.

bag that is closest to the tree trunk. Water naturally exits a tree from time to time, and when it does it will remain in the bag to be collected later.

Making a **solar still** is another means of collecting water from vegetation or a dirty water source. This method will require a little more work, but if you are staying in an area for a few days it may be worth your while to make one. Dig a hole into the ground that will be slightly smaller in length and width than the piece of plastic you have. Using the wood saw or knife, cut a large pile of green vegetation and stack it into the hole. Create a small space in the middle of the vegetation where a collecting device—a cup—can be placed. Spread the plastic across the hole and anchor the edges with rocks.

Place a small rock in the middle of the plastic so that the plastic is pulled down several inches from ground level. This low point should be placed directly over the container that is collecting the water. This structure will create a greenhouse effect. As the chamber in the ground heats up, water will leave the vegetation. Through evaporation, the moisture will travel upward and be trapped by the plastic. When enough water is collected to form drops, the water will travel to the lowest point on the plastic and fall into the cup. If you don't have a cup, use the Swiss Army Knife to carve out a depression in a piece of wood. Collecting any amount of water from

> *"Architects cannot teach nature anything."*
> —Mark Twain

this method can take several hours, if not most of the day, so set it up early.

Here is another method for creating a solar still. This is going to require the use of two different containers: a 2-liter plastic bottle and a bottle or container that is small enough to fit inside the 2-liter bottle. Make a cut into the two-liter bottle just below the neck so that the top can be removed. Place the other container that is filled with dirty water inside the 2-liter bottle. Replace the top so that it is on the inside of the bottle. Place this whole contraption in a sunny location. As it heats up, water will evaporate from the smaller container, travel upward, and be trapped inside the 2-liter bottle. As the moisture builds up, it will form drops of water that will travel downward and collect in the bottom of the plastic bottle.

Taking advantage of **rainfall** is a great way to refill water containers quickly. Use a collector with the largest surface area possible in order to funnel the water into a container. This will allow a greater quantity of water to be collected faster. Stringing up a tarp or plastic bag are great options as collectors. If there are extra plastic bottles at your disposal, cut the top off of one just below the neck, but keep the piece that has been cut off. This will allow you to use the body of the plastic bottle as one collector and invert the piece that was cut off to use as a funnel in another bottle that may have a smaller bottle opening.

Cleaning Water

Finding water is not enough; we also have to make it drinkable. This can be done by filtering, boiling, distillation, or the addition of chemical additives.

DISTILLATION

If you happen to be near an extremely dirty water source or salt water, the Swiss Army Knife can help you to purify water by making a simple distiller. Heat the salt/dirty water until it creates steam. When the steam is cooled, it forms into water droplets and is collected. Salt and many other contaminants are left behind in the dirty container, while much cleaner water will be in the collection container.

There are many different setups and materials that one can use. You will need some kind of container in which to boil the water, a piece of tubing that the steam will be transferred through, and a collection container.

I used a clear glass bottle I found as the dirty water container. When using a container of unknown origin, you don't know exactly what was in it prior to your finding it. If there is water to spare, fill the container and rinse it out three times. Once that is done, use the knife to cut a piece of plastic tubing to length and jam it into the mouth of the bottle. Because you don't want the bottle to become overly hot and potentially melt the plastic tubing, place the base of the bottle on the outer perimeter of your fire. (This is why one would ideally use metal, such as copper, for the tubing.) The less heat directed at the bottle, the slower the process, but I can always whittle something while I am waiting.

As the water heats up, the steam will rise and travel through the tubing. In the tubing, the steam should cool enough that it condenses and forms water droplets, collecting in the container below. If you find that the steam is escaping from the end of the tubing because it is not cooling, wrap a damp rag around the tubing to help cool it down. The rag may need to be doused with water several times throughout the process in order to keep it cool—take care that the water from the rag doesn't run down into the collecting container!

Metal tubing would be ideal, but sometimes you have to use whatever you can find.

WATER FILTER

Knowing how to make a water filter so that you have access to clean water could mean the difference between life and death. There are many different ways to filter and clean water, but here is a method where the supplies used would be the most likely ones available in the outdoors. I have used this method to clean "dirty-looking" water, filtering out debris such as silt, grass, insects, soil, etc. I highly recommend that the water collected from this filter still be boiled or purified by means of purification chemicals.

Using the knife of your Swiss Army Knife, cut the bottom off a 2-liter plastic bottle. Tie a coffee filter or handkerchief around the outside opening of the bottle with a rubber band or a piece of cordage. Fold this last layer of the filter onto itself several times; this slows down the water drip but increases the last filter step. Invert the bottle and start layering in the material that will filter the water. Place layers of charcoal, sand, small rocks, and then medium rocks.

Pour the dirty water over the rocks on the top layer of the filter. Even when the water looks "clean," I always recommend cleaning it further by boiling or placing chemical additives in the water.

Finding, collecting, and cleaning water can take time, and thirst can be overpowering. Remain patient, for the smallest drink of contaminated water can make you very ill. Unclean water sources may contain parasites, viruses, and bacteria. Consuming or coming into contact with these pathogens can cause diseases such as cholera and dysentery. These diseases can be particularly deadly in a survival situation, as they cause vomiting and diarrhea and leave the body severely dehydrated.

As charcoal is one of the smallest filters in this project, having a larger layer of that will be important.

Here is the dirty water that I started with. Looks delicious, doesn't it?

Here is what the water looks like from the top of the filter. There is a lot of large debris that will be filtered out in the top portion of the filter.

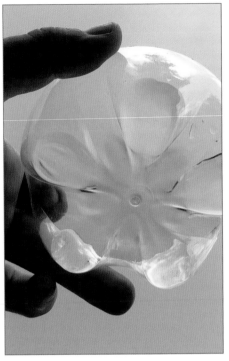

The bottom that I cut off of the 2-liter bottle serves as a collecting container. As you can see, there is quite a difference between the original water and the water that is collected.

Here is a side view of the water filter. The large debris, such as silt and grass, will be filtered out by the larger items on top, the rocks and sand. As the water travels through the filter, smaller and smaller items contained in the water will be filtered out.

Grooming

Hair Trimming

We have all been there: you have missed a few days of taking care of your personal appearance. Maybe you forgot to shave, trim your nails, or get a haircut. When this goes on too long, we tend to feel a bit off and not like ourselves. Believe it or not, personal grooming can be a psychological boost because it shows that we are taking care of ourselves. Anything that will boost your morale in a difficult situation will be beneficial to you.

The scissors on the Swiss Army Knife are very sharp and make an effective cutting tool. It might take some time, but they work well in trimming your hair or beard. I also like to use the scissors to trim the beard hairs around my mouth, as this tool is precise and works well in small areas.

Don't worry about packing a mirror to check your progress, as the highly polished surfaces on the Swiss Army Knife tools have a mirror finish.

I think I have earned those white hairs in my beard.

"Nature is the art of God."
—Dante Alghieri

Nail Care

Keeping your nails trimmed is important. Longer nails can harbor bacteria under them and are more likely to snag onto something, which can contribute to an injury. Without a nail clipper, the nail file may be used for smoothing out nails after they are cut with the scissors. File the nail in one direction to prevent snags.

In the absence of medical care or proper hygiene methods, we need to avoid even the smallest tears in our skin to avoid infections. Rather than picking hangnails and risking the chance open cuts, I now use the scissors to remove them.

Brushing Your Teeth

Brushing your teeth is another one of those tasks that can be easily overlooked in an outdoor situation. A whole host of health problems can arise from a lack of dental care. To prevent this, use the wood saw to cut a small branch or twig from a tree. Softer woods such as pine tend to work best. Place the end of the twig into your mouth and chew it up until the wood fibers are bristle-like.

Now comes the tasty part. Take some charcoal from your fire and grind it up in a cup. Add just enough water to make a paste. This will act as your toothpaste. Dip the chewed-up end of the twig into the charcoal paste and polish away! Make sure that you

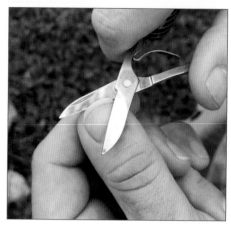

I almost prefer using the scissors over a nail clipper because they work so well.

have some clean water handy to rinse out your mouth, as the paste is gritty and tastes a bit odd. And don't forget that the toothpick will help clean food particles from the tight spaces between those pearly whites.

Flossing

Brushing isn't always enough. Did you know that you can floss your teeth with paracord? Use the scissors tool to snip off an end of paracord, exposing the inner strands. Pull out one of the strands, and cut it when you have the length you want. These inner strands can be further pulled apart to produce even finer strands that work great as dental floss.

Gear Repair

Gear and clothes are not going to last forever, and at some point they will get a rip in them. There are many tools in the Swiss Army Knife that will make repairing items possible, and even a breeze. The reamer is the go-to tool for sewing through large and tough material, such as leather and canvas.

Sometimes, though, there are situations where having a more traditional needle would be advantageous. There is a variety of material a needle could be made from: a thorn from a plant, bone, or even a piece of wood. I made a large wood needle by using the reamer to "drill" a hole in one end and the small knife to create the point at the other. This could be used for larger projects such as net repair.

A needle can also be improvised with a spring from the scissors or pliers. Straighten the spring and sharpen the point to your satisfaction. The other end of the spring already has a small eye on it, which is nice for threading cordage through.

There are times when an article of clothing or some other material may need to be sacrificed in order to be used for the greater good. To separate material so that it can be reused, the reamer works as an improvised seam ripper. It is thin enough to squeeze into tight spaces and pry material apart, and the

sharp blade can cut the original seam. I have used the can opener for this purpose, but the reamer works better. If the fabric is a light color, I also like to use the ballpoint pen to outline where I will be sewing.

> *"The best view comes after the hardest climb."*
> **—Anonymous**

Helpful Modifications

While the reamer does a good job of sewing, I like to have a traditional sewing needle with my gear. I found that if you remove the toothpick, which is my least-utilized tool, a sewing needle fits in this space nicely. Depending on the needle's size, it may need to be secured with a small piece of tape. If the toothpick is a must-have, the needle can always be taped onto the scales of the knife. I like larger needles because they are easier to handle, so I secured mine on the outside of the scales. Other than its obvious use, the needle can be used as a makeshift compass needle and for first aid.

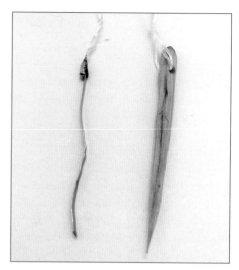

The spring is a bit flimsy but still strong enough to push through most material. The wood needle has a "soft" point but is easy to make.

In My Experience

The tools in the Swiss Army Knife can help in maintaining and fine-tuning other pieces of equipment. Recently a friend of mine gifted me a fixed-blade knife that I had had my eye on for quite some time. The other day while I was out and about, I started to use the knife and noticed that the scales (handles) felt a little loose. Normally I would carry my SwissChamp with me, but something was different that morning. When I woke up, I decided to mix things up a bit and carry my SwissChamp XLT instead. The XLT model comes with a bit wrench and several bits. Luckily it contained a bit that fit perfectly into the hardware that I needed to tighten on my fixed-blade knife. Thanks to the Swiss Army Knife, I was able to go about my day.

 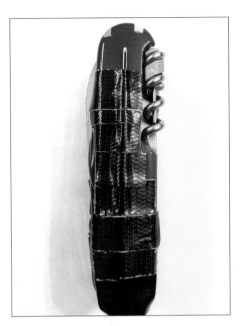

Make sure that you use strong tape such as duct tape.

A WORD OF ADVICE

When gear becomes so damaged that it is beyond our ability to repair it, don't just discard it. Repurpose everything you can. This is especially important in a survival situation where you can't just walk down to your local store for materials.

A backpack is a common item that people carry that can be broken down into many usable parts if needed. Smaller zippered sections can be cut out in such a way to create pouches that can be carried. The shoulder straps can be removed and used as shoulder straps on a newly made pack. Straps and webbing can be removed and used as cordage. Pieces of the pack material can be cut out to be used as sewing patches or to help filter water. Buckles can be used with cordage to make straps, slings, belts, and handles. So the next time a piece of gear appears to be done for, take a second look at it.

FLASHLIGHT POUCH

What You Will Need

- **Material for the pouch**
- **Sewing cordage** (inner strands of paracord in this project)
- **Reamer with sewing eye**
- **Small piece of wood**
- **Paracord**
- **Scissors**
- **Lighter**

ESTIMATED TIME FOR PROJECT

1 hour

You can make a belt holster for your flashlight in order make it more accessible. And you can make it by using only the materials that you would probably have if you were away from home. The inner strands of the paracord are going to be used for the sewing thread, while the whole piece of paracord will be used for some finishing touches.

1. To use the inner strands of paracord, cut the cord and simply pull out the number of strands needed. In this instance, I had two different widths of straps. Use the smaller strap as the belt loop on the back of the holster. The larger straps can be used for the main body of the holster. Lay the larger straps alongside a flashlight to estimate how much is needed. I took two of the thicker pieces of nylon straps and sewed them together side by side. This was done twice, producing one set for the front and one set for the back.

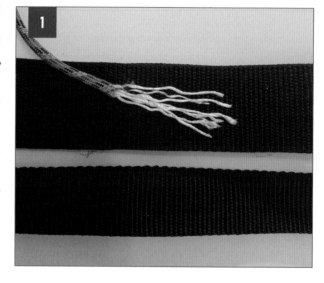

2. Overlap the straps slightly when sewing them.

3. With the reamer tool extended, insert one end of a piece of cordage (inner strands of paracord, twine, jute twine, etc.) into the sewing eye at the end of the blade. Make sure there are several inches of cordage pulled through. Burning the end of the inner strand will help when threading it through the sewing eye.

4. Push the reamer through the material. Depending on the material you are attaching together, leather for instance, you may have to push quite hard. Be careful not to have any part of your body behind where the reamer will come through. When the reamer has been pushed through and the sewing eye is on the opposite side of the material, pull an excess amount of the cordage through the sewing eye. Always use more cord than you think you might need.

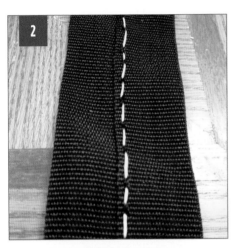

5. Remove the reamer from the first hole while leaving one end of the cordage that was pushed through. Move the reamer to the next position and push it through the material. As the reamer is pulled back slightly, the cordage should make a small loop above the sewing eye. Take the end of the cordage and pull it through this loop. Be mindful not to inadvertently cut the cord on the reamer edge.

6. Hold onto the end of the cordage that was pulled through the loop as the reamer is pulled backward. Tug both ends of the cordage to tighten the connection that was just made. Repeat this process until you get to the end of the line. Having only one stitch on the belt loop keeps it fairly loose.

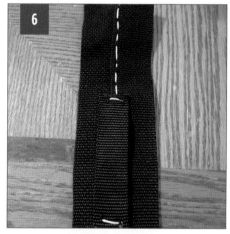

7. To finish, cut the excess cordage against the blade of the reamer. Tie two knots and burn the end of the cordage, if applicable. Nylon cordage will melt and help seal the end, but twine, like jute, will just burn.

Before attaching the front and back pieces, I took the smaller strap and sewed it onto the back for a belt loop.

Now that you have a pouch for your flashlight, you don't want the flashlight to fall out. Here's a simple way to close the pouch.

- Cut a small piece of wood using the wood saw and thread paracord through a hole in the wood that was drilled with the reamer.
- Push the other end of the paracord through two holes in the top flap and tie off.
- To create the loop, make two holes in the lower portion of the holster and thread paracord through it. Tie it off on the inside of the holster.
- When the top flap is closed, push the piece of wood through the loop and the flap will stay shut.

If you don't like the previous sewing method, you can still use the reamer to punch holes in the material and create the desired sewing pattern. Here is one method to use the reamer that is a bit easier.

- Overlap the two materials you wish to attach.
- Place the cordage into the sewing eye of the reamer and press the reamer through both materials.
- Pull the cord out of the sewing eye and retract the reamer.
- Move the reamer to the next spot on the material and press it through both pieces of material.
- Thread a few inches (centimeters) of cordage through the sewing eye and pull the reamer back through the material.
- Move to the next position and push the reamer through the material.
- Remove the thread from the sewing eye and pull the reamer back through the material.
- Repeat this process to the end of the seam and knot the end.

Always thinking outside the box will help you come up with useful and fun projects like this.

REPAIRING A SHEATH

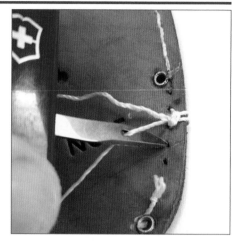

Sometimes the reamer can make larger holes than you want
when using the sewing eye. If the holes in the material are smaller
and you want to keep them that way, simply use the tip of the
reamer to push the cordage through.

While the Swiss Army Knife is incredibly
useful, there are other tools that I carry on
me when I am out. One of those is a hatchet
or an axe. And just like the Swiss Army Knife,
it is important to protect that tool with a
sheath. Through wear and tear, a sheath can
start to split or come apart along the edges.
Pictured here is the leather sheath that I
use to cover and protect the head of my axe.
Some of the threading started to come out,
so I repaired it using the tools in my Swiss
Army Knife.

The first thing I did was cut and removed
any of the remaining thread along the sewing
line. I used the tip of the reaming tool to pry
the thread up, and the scissors to cut it. From
here I used the same sewing method used
in the preceding flashlight pouch project to
shore up the edges of my leather sheath. This
repair method can be used for an assortment
of coverings and sheaths.

A WORD OF ADVICE

Always use protective coverings
for your tools. Our tools will take
care of us as long as we take
care of them. When properly
cared for, a tool can last a long
time.

IMPROVISED GLOVES

What You Will Need

- **Material for the gloves**
- **Cordage for sewing**
- **Reamer with sewing eye**
- **Scissors or knife**

ESTIMATED TIME FOR PROJECT

30 minutes

It is easy to take things for granted and not really appreciate them until they are gone. There have been a few times when I incurred injuries to my hands that incapacitated one of them for a period of time. I couldn't believe how frustrating even the simplest tasks were when I could only use one hand. If an injury such as that ever happened and I was on the move in a dire situation, it could spell big trouble. Sometimes even the smallest injury, like a splinter or cut, can cause serious problems if proper treatment is not available. I always recommend having a pair of gloves in your go-bag or vehicle for this reason. However, if you find yourself without gloves, you can rough out a pair as long as you have your trusty Swiss Army Knife!

Using strong material such as canvas or leather would be best, but when times are tough, use any material you can find. For this project I used denim because it is a fairly tough material that is easy to work with. For added protection I made these gloves arm-length, which was easy since I used pant legs for the body of the glove.

Here I am wearing my pants gloves, getting ready to carve on this piece of wood.

- First get your measurements. To do this, stick your hand through the bottom of the pant leg and pull it up to your bicep. There is more material in the thigh section of pants, which will be saved for the fingers of the glove.
- After stretching out the material where your hand will be, cut the pant leg straight across about a couple of inches (centimeters) above your fingers with the scissors. Always cut a bit more material than you think you are going to need; you can always trim off the excess later.
- Cut the seams of the pants on one side with the scissors and lay them on a flat surface so that the inside of the denim faces up.
- Lay your arm and hand onto the material and use the pen to make a tracing (if you have a Swiss Army Knife model with a pen).
- After tracing, cut the remaining seam down the middle of the pant leg.
- With the tracing of your hand facing up, lay the tracing on top of the other pant leg.
- From here it is just a matter of sewing. Use the same method utilized in the flashlight pouch project (page 188) to sew the material together.

- Wait until after the sewing is done to trim the perimeter and between the fingers.

In My Experience

I remember one bad day when I broke and lost quite a few of the loops on a pair of my shoes. I took an old pair of jeans and used the knife on the Swiss Army Knife to cut the belt loops from the waistline. From there I folded the pieces in half to create a loop and sewed the ends with the pin from my Swiss Army Knife. The ends of the loop were then pressed back into the opening of the shoe with the tip of the reamer and sewed into place. This was quite difficult and tedious work with the pin and tip of the reamer, but I got the job done and the loops have held up well.

These four denim loops have lasted me for almost a year now!

Repairing Shoes/Boots

Foot care is extremely important. If you can't walk, then you are dead in the water, so to speak. I have had shoes and boots fail me on a number of occasions. Two of the most common things are laces breaking and the lace loops breaking.

The laces are an easy fix if you have extra cordage. Cut to length and thread through the shoe loops. With most of my outdoor shoes and boots, I tend to take the original laces out and replace them with 550 paracord. After cutting the paracord to length, make sure to burn and seal the ends. I keep the original laces in my pack as a backup.

If the lace loops break but you still have the material from the loop, use the reamer or pin to sew the loop back into the shoe.

Pin Sewing

Some models, such as the SwissChamp, come with a very small pin that can be used as an improvised sewing needle. This works great for smaller sewing jobs that the reamer is just too big for. Since the pin is very little, it will require small thread. The back of the pin has a small top to it, so the pin won't go through material as easily as a regular needle would.

A WORD OF ADVICE

Within the buckle of a belt is the pin that fits into the hole of the belt. I have had this pin become severely bent and even break on me before. A bent pin is easily fixed by bending it back into place with the pliers or using other tools as a leverage point to bend the metal. If the pin breaks, all is not lost. An improvised pin may be made out of a piece of wood. This will require a small piece of wood and a bit of cordage. There may be a small bit of the old pin still on the buckle that needs to be removed. Use any of the tools available to remove that last bit of metal.

Split the piece of wood on one end so that it can go around the buckle where the old pin was. The frame of the buckle should rest in the split between the two pieces of wood. Secure the cut end of the wood to the buckle by wrapping it with cordage. This should be wrapped tightly, but if done correctly it should allow the pin to pivot. On the opposite end of this piece, use the small knife to carve away enough wood so that it will fit into the holes of the belt. This fix will not last forever, but it should last long enough until a new piece of metal can be obtained to replace the pin.

Taking It Down a Notch

The reamer tool can be used to create new holes in leather belts. Take the reamer, press down on the leather, and rotate all the way around until a hole has been created. When one side is done, use the reamer on the opposite side to clean it up a bit. Being able to create new holes in a belt or strap will help to size a tourniquet if the need should arise in an emergency medical situation.

When a new belt hole is needed, use the reamer tool.

Knots

Knowing how to tie a variety of knots is a great skill to have. Just as important is knowing how to untie them. I have had my fair share of knots that were so tight that there seemed to be no possibility of loosening them in this lifetime. Most of the time frustration took over and I simply cut the cordage. I have thrown away many shoelaces because of this—that is, until I learned a little trick. The corkscrew on the Swiss Army Knife can also be used to loosen impossible knots. The sharp tip easily slips in between the pieces of cordage. Rotate the spiral of the corkscrew and wiggle it around. The tension in the knot will soon be much more manageable.

If your Swiss Army Knife model doesn't have a hook tool, the corkscrew can help in improvising a handle. Using preexisting knots, rotate the corkscrew so that the bundle of knots is all the way at the base. The cordage and corkscrew will sit between your fingers as the Swiss Army Knife frame acts as a handle.

Inserting the corkscrew into the last loop will help loosen and pull the end of the cordage.

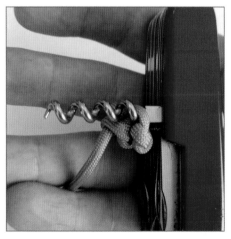

This is a quick way to grip cordage without hurting your hands.

A WORD OF ADVICE

The marlin spike and the shackle opener are other great tools for loosening stubborn knots.

ZIPPER PULL HANDLE

What You Will Need

- **Key ring from Swiss Army Knife**
- **Paracord**
- **Scissors or knife**
- **Lighter**

ESTIMATED TIME FOR PROJECT

15 minutes

1. Take a small length of paracord and double it through the key ring. This will be the "body" in which I will be braiding around. Take a longer piece of paracord, around a few feet (about a meter), and find the middle of it. Place the middle of this cord around the back of the body. Since the key ring on the Swiss Army Knife is on the smaller side, remove the inner strands from the paracord to make it fit better inside the ring.

Having the zipper handle break off a bag, tent flap, or coat can be quite infuriating. If you have your Swiss Army Knife on you, then there is a very simple fix. Remove the key ring from the frame of the Swiss Army Knife. Bend one of the ends of the ring so that it can be threaded onto the zipper frame. Turn the ring until it is fully seated. Tie or braid a few pieces of paracord or other cordage to the ring, and you now have a new zipper pull. The spring from the scissors or pliers can also be used, but I don't advise it—the trade-off of tool efficiency for a simple fix is unwise.

The key ring solution will last until a new zipper can be installed. I have another method I used for a winter coat when its zipper handle broke off. It lasted for almost two years! Here's how to make a cobra weave braid out of paracord to use for the handle.

2. Place the left side of the cord over the top of the body and under the right side of the cord.

3. Take the right cord and go under the left cord, behind the body, and up and through the loop that was created. It's okay if the two inner strands that make up the body twist at the top, but keep them straight after this step.

4. Pull the left and right side of the cord to tighten the knot. Don't press the first knot all the way to the top. Leave a small loop so that the paracord can easily be moved around the ring when you are finished.

5. The next steps remain the same, except alternating from right to left. To make the next knot, start with the cord on the right side and fold it over the body.

6. Take the left side of the cord and go under the right cord, behind the body, and up and through the loop that was created. The size of the knots and how you want the pattern to look will determine how tight you make the knots.

7. Pull the left and right sides of the cord to tighten the knot. The inner strand will form a V pattern as you progress.

8. Repeat the preceding steps until the zipper pull has reached the desired length. As the braid progresses, press it slightly upward to create a smooth pattern without gaps.

9. When you are done braiding, it's time to take out the Swiss Army Knife scissors, which give a much cleaner cut than the knife would. Cut the left and right cords a few inches (centimeters) away from the body.

10. Use a lighter to burn and melt the cut end of the cord. Be careful, because the burning nylon will be hot and sticky. Use the side of the lighter to press the soft nylon down into the side of the knot. If the black edges are too rough for your liking, warm them up with the lighter and carefully smooth them out with your thumb.

11. The two strands hanging out of the end can be tied in a knot or left as is. Cut them and burn the ends. Your zipper pull handle is now ready to be attached.

Eyeglasses & Watches

In some Swiss Army Knife models there is a miniature screwdriver that resides within the corkscrew. This tool is ideal for tightening the screws on eyeglasses and making adjustments to watches. It also works as a small pry bar for taking the back off a watch, for pushing out tiny pins, or for removing small batteries without damaging the housing. The miniature screwdriver also helps remove and replace the springs of the scissors and pliers.

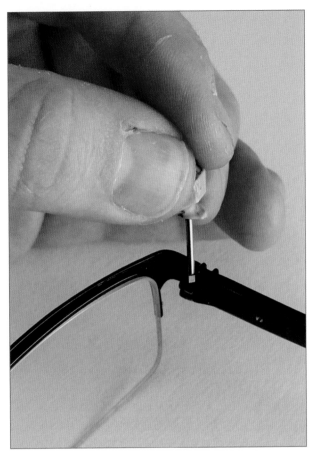

This screwdriver fits perfectly into the hardware of my glasses.

Gear Repair

Firearm Maintenance

I grew up spending a lot of time around firearms. It is not always possible to carry all of the tools on you that you might need, so I learned early on to utilize the Swiss Army Knife. What follows are general techniques that can be used with your Swiss Army Knife. No specific firearm model or procedure is referenced due to the variety of firearms available.

Many firearms can be taken apart with the removal of a few pins or other hardware. The punch, the reamer, the Phillips screwdriver, the tip of the file, and the miniature screwdriver work well to push those pins out.

When using metal tools on your firearm, it is always a good idea to place a piece of fabric between the tool and the firearm. This will help protect the firearm's finish.

In My Experience

A day of hunting was almost ruined for me when I took a spill while walking in the woods. My long gun went barrel first into the ground, compacting half of the barrel with mud. I unloaded the firearm and, utilizing this cleaning method, I was able to clear the barrel of all debris.

There are a lot of small spaces in firearms where dirt, powder residue, and any other type of foreign debris will find its way in. The small tools on a Swiss Army Knife work perfectly with a cleaning cloth to get into those hard-to-reach places. The tip of the bottle opener and can opener help slide cleaning patches into tight spaces.

When the bore needs to be cleaned, drop a length of paracord through one end and tie off the other end to a cleaning patch. I tend

The skinny tools, like the openers and reamer, work great in tight spaces.

The scissors are great for cutting the right size cleaning patches to wipe away that grime. These are patches that I cut from an old cotton T-shirt.

Most hunters don't carry a firearm cleaning kit on them, which is why this technique comes in handy.

Firearm Maintenance

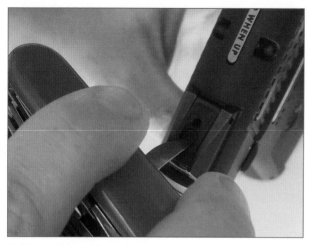

The Swiss Army Knife can help you stay on target every time. Here, I am using the small flathead screwdriver to adjust my rear sight.

to make my patches on the large side so that they really rub against the sides of the barrel. If the patch is difficult to pull through, simply tie off one end of the paracord to the hook attachment to give you a better grip.

On a long gun such as a shotgun, use the bottle opener to unscrew the cap in order to gain access to the tube that contains the plug. I usually have a sling on my long guns. There are tools in the Swiss Army Knife that can be used to adjust some of the sling hardware or remove it completely. There have been a number of times when I have had some of the sling hardware become so loose I thought it was going to come out. I used my Swiss Army Knife to tighten the hardware so that I could continue to use the sling without causing any damage to the firearm.

"We don't inherit the earth from our ancestors, we borrow it from our children."
—David Brower

The "skinner" medium models work best for this, as the frame of the knife will fit further into the tube.

First Aid

Whenever possible, a person should always carry, at minimum, a small first aid kit when spending time outdoors. However, I realize that we can suddenly be thrust into situations where we do not have the luxuries of certain supplies. There are many plants that can be used for medicinal purposes, but make sure that you are well versed in plant identification before attempting their use.

Accidents do happen, but the first step in keeping yourself free of injuries is prevention. Being safety conscious at all times is going to reduce your need for first aid. Here are some tips for keeping safe when in the field. Some of these tips require having certain supplies, while others do not.

Wear sunglasses or some form of eye protection (see the improvised sunglasses project on page 122) when walking through the woods or areas of thick vegetation.

Walk slowly and deliberately while continuously scanning the area. Unless you are in immediate danger, you need to slow down in order to notice hazards around you. You need to be aware of potential dangers

In My Experience

One day I tripped and fell onto a very thorny tree. A thorn cut into my face, barely missing my eye. Ever since then, I always carry my sunglasses or a pair of safety glasses/goggles in my pack.

above you as well as those at ground level. Those things are hard to notice if you are moving too fast through an area.

Also **be aware of your footing**. Don't step over large objects like a log or rock, but rather step onto them. You may not be able to see what is on the other side of the object before stepping over it. There could be a hole in the ground or an animal at rest that you could frighten. This is especially important to remember in poisonous snake country! Taking such a large step over an object would also throw your balance off. Always test your footing each time a step is taken when crossing rocky, snowy, or wet terrain. A wet or mossy rock can be as slick as ice.

Keep your skin covered as much as possible to prevent minor cuts when walking through thick vegetation. The smallest of tears in the skin can lead to infections and big problems down the road.

Speaking of keeping yourself covered, don't forget about your hands! We obviously use our hands a lot, so protect them as much as possible by wearing gloves. There are times when gloves can be a bit inhibiting, but I strongly recommend using them as much as possible.

Splinters

Other than making fire, the magnifying glass has come in handy when trying to locate the many splinters that have found their way into my skin over the years. A small splinter in the right spot can be distracting and painful, and could cause an infection. The magnifying glass coupled with the toothpick, pin, or tweezers make easy work of removing splinters.

There are times when it doesn't matter what kind of tweezers are being used; just getting a grip on the end of the splinter can be difficult. Use one side of the tweezers and place it under the end of the splinter that is sticking out. Using another finger, press the splinter from the back end. The tweezers will help to guide the splinter up and out rather than being pressed further into the skin.

The pliers work well to remove larger foreign objects, because some splinters can be quite large. I recall a time when I

In My Experience

When I was in my teens I took a summer job detasseling corn but didn't wear a long-sleeve shirt like everyone else. I ignored the stinging sensation I felt throughout the day. When I left, I discovered that the leaves of the cornstalks had made tiny cuts all over my arms. Not long after, I started to have an allergic reaction to something and my arms swelled up like balloons. Keep yourself covered!

was trying to break a branch in half and a piece of wood—roughly the diameter of a pencil—conveniently jammed itself under my thumbnail. Because of how the wood was situated and because of all the blood, I could not get a good grip on it with my other hand. The pliers of my SwissChamp saved the day, as I used them to grip and pull out the chunk of wood.

Blisters

Generally speaking, I don't pop blisters unless they are severely inhibiting due to location on the body or if they become too painful. The fluid contained in the blister helps to protect the new skin contained below. If you are intent on popping a blister, don't just rip it open. It is better to drain it. Use the smallest puncturing tool you have. The pin on the SwissChamp works well. Sterilize the pin with hand sanitizer or expose it to a flame for several seconds. Puncture a small hole near the base of the blister, then gently squeeze the blister to drain the fluid out. Once all of the fluid has been drained, apply a bandage to cover and protect the skin. Wait a few days before uncovering it.

> *"I love nature. I just don't want to get any of it on me."*
> **—Woody Allen**

Ticks

One of the best ways to remove a tick that has dug its nasty little teeth into you is to burn it with a blown-out match or the tweezer tool heated by fire. This causes the tick to release its bite from the skin, leaving no doubt about whether any part of the tick remains embedded in the skin.

Swollen Finger

There is one thing I will always have on me no matter where I am or what I am doing: my wedding ring. But there are some limited situations where wearing jewelry can pose a safety risk. I once smashed my hand, causing my ring finger to swell up. Wearing a ring on a finger that is swelling up can be incredibly uncomfortable and painful—plus it will cut off circulation to the finger. I don't recall where I learned this, but there is an ingenious trick to removing a ring from an enlarged finger.

Would you believe me if I said all you needed were a piece of small cordage and tweezers? Cut an inner strand of paracord several feet (a meter or so) long. Use the tweezers to gently push one end of the paracord under the ring toward the base of your finger. Pull just a few inches (centimeters) through. Begin wrapping the remaining paracord around your finger toward the tip. Hold onto the end of cord that was pushed under the ring and begin pulling it toward the tip of the finger. As the cord is pulled, it unwinds around your finger and pulls the ring off.

Making a Squirt Bottle to Clean a Wound

Keeping a cut in the skin clean is an essential step in preventing an infection, especially when the injury first happens. Using clean water with a little bit of pressure behind it will help wash any foreign debris from a wound. A very simple spray bottle can be made from a plastic water bottle. With the reamer, cut a hole in the center of the bottle cap. I like using the reamer over the knife for this task because it creates a nice round hole. This will produce a much stronger stream of water that can be directed more accurately. After the hole has been made, fill the bottle up with clean water and squeeze.

Removing a Fishhook

There is nothing that stops a good fishing day in its tracks like having a fishhook sunk into your skin. The common areas in which I have had hooks stuck include the legs, arms, hands, ears—and even my face a few times. Most of the time the hooks were only in my skin superficially, so they were easy to remove by simply pulling them out. However, there were a few times when the hooks went quite a bit deeper. A deeply sunk fishhook has to be dealt with differently because of the barb at the end of it. If I tried to pull a barbed hook straight out of my skin, I'd cause a lot of tissue damage. The barb is going to grab onto anything it can as the hook is pulled. To avoid this, here are two techniques for removing a barbed hook.

CUT THE BARB OFF

If you are lucky and the hook has gone in and completely through the skin, the barb can be cut off. To accomplish this, cut off the end of the hook with the Swiss Army Knife's metal saw, or use the metal file to file down the barb until it is smooth. The hook can then be gently pulled back out.

Sometimes the hook doesn't go all the way through the skin. When this happens, you may have to cause yourself a little more pain by pushing the hook through the skin in order to expose the barb. While this is painful, it should cause less damage to the tissue than trying to back the hook out. Once the barb is exposed, cut it off as detailed above.

BACK THE HOOK OUT

This method is more effective with smaller hooks because the barb is smaller. However, even if a small hook has gone all the way through the skin, I recommend removing the barb and taking the hook out as discussed. If the small hook is embedded in the skin, backing it out can be attempted.

To do this, the hook needs to be gently pressed down toward the skin, but not in such a way that the hook pierces further into the tissue. This helps to keep the barb from grabbing onto too much tissue as the hook is pulled out. With small hooks, it may be difficult to grip them with your fingers. To help in pulling them out, wrap a thin piece of cordage or fishing line around the hook. The pliers can also be used. While pushing the hook down, use the string or pliers to gently pull the hook out.

Immobilizing

Unfortunately, there may come a time when a body part is injured to a degree that it needs to be immobilized. This can take the form of a jammed finger, sprained ankle, or a broken bone. Here are some ways to use the Swiss Army Knife to create materials to aid in such injuries.

The wood saw or knife can be used to cut small branches for finger splints. Tape, cordage, handkerchief, or bandana can be used to wrap the splints in place around a finger. With larger pieces of wood, this same technique can be used to immobilize a leg or an arm.

If a leg injury occurs, it would take less effort and provide more comfort to use a crutch over a walking stick. This may be difficult to acquire if walking is painful, but try to find a branch that is thick enough to support your body and has a Y shape at some point. Use the wood saw to remove any side branches that could become a sharp hazard in case of a fall, and wrap any extra clothing into the Y for cushioning against your body.

Making a Tourniquet

There are times when things can go south very quickly. If you are need of a tourniquet, you may have to act fast. Tourniquets should only be used in extreme circumstances, as prolonged use can cause further damage.

A tourniquet is a strap that is applied above a wound site in order to slow or stop excessive blood loss. It can be made from almost anything: a bootlace, vines, cordage, an article of clothing, straps from a pack, or a belt. In the section on gear repair (page 196), I show how to use the reamer tool to make holes in a belt to adjust it. Since many of us

First Aid

wear a belt, it would be quick and easy to use one for a tourniquet.

If material such as cordage, bootlaces, or a handkerchief is being used, it may be difficult to tighten. Tie off the ends of the material to the Swiss Army Knife, and use the Swiss Army Knife to twist the material in order to tighten it.

Amputation

I cannot personally attest to using the Swiss Army Knife in this manner, thank goodness. Here are a few real-life situations in which multi-tools were used to this degree.

I recently read the book *127 Hours: Between a Rock and a Hard Place* by Aron Ralston. It's the true story of how Ralston, an experienced outdoorsman, was out on a day hike in the canyons of Utah when tragedy struck. A large boulder he had just stepped on was dislodged and pinned his arm to the canyon wall. For five days he tried various methods to free his arm, but nothing worked. On his fifth day without food or water, Aron did the unthinkable. He broke his arm and used a multi-tool (not a Swiss Army Knife but a multi-tool with similar tools) to amputate his arm below the elbow in order to free himself. After wrapping his arm in a makeshift tourniquet, Aron walked several miles before being found by a family, leading to his rescue. This is a harrowing tale of self-rescue and a testament to the human will to survive.

In the 1990s, while based in Uganda, a Canadian surgeon used his Swiss Army Knife to perform amputations because his saw had been stolen. (Check out the article at *https://www.nytimes.com/2008/01/10/business/worldbusiness/10iht-10swiss.9120162.html.*)

Pretty gruesome to imagine, but when we have nothing else to lose and are on the verge of death, we will do anything to survive or save someone else. I sincerely hope that anyone who is reading this will never have to go through such an ordeal. But if you do, take heart in knowing that the wood saw, metal saw, and knife on the Swiss Army Knife are sufficient tools to complete such a task.

More Uses for Your Swiss Army Knife

In this section I won't be talking about projects, but rather about some uses of the Swiss Army Knife tools that sometimes go overlooked—or ways in which to use the tools that you may not have thought of.

For the longest time I did not know what that little notch on the base of the bottle opener was, so I just ignored it. I later found out that it is a small **wire stripper**, and I find it very interesting how they integrated it. Extend the bottle opener so that it is perpendicular to the frame, and then open up the large knife blade. Place the wire in the notch, and press the knife down so that the cutting edge is touching the wire insulation where you want to cut. The downward pressure of the knife is enough that it will hold that end of the wire in place. Lightly hold onto the notched end while spinning the Swiss Army Knife with your other hand. Use the notch to then help pull the insulation from the wire. If the wire is too large for the notch, use the large blade to cut the insulation as mentioned above.

"Nature does not hurry, yet everything is accomplished."
—Lao Tzu

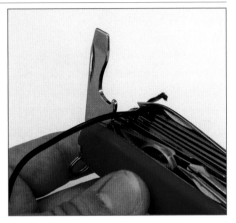

After the cut has been made, pull the wire back and use the notch to pull the insulation where the cut has been made.

In My Experience

One time when I was out hunting, I felt something sharp on the bottom of my foot. I just figured that a small rock or something had found its way into my shoe, so I decided to keep walking. After about five minutes I had to stop and remove my shoe. It turned out that, while walking through fields and the woods, I had somehow managed to step on a nail. I didn't have a pair of pliers, so I used the bottle opener on my Swiss Army Knife to dig in around the head of the nail until I could lift it slightly away from the tread of the boot. I then placed the wire stripper notch onto the shaft of the nail and pried it out, much like you would with the claw of a hammer. Removing nails like this also works around the house when your wife decides she wants to rearrange all of the pictures.

The **bottle opener** can also be used as a mini pry bar, but be careful how much force you use. I have mainly used it to remove small nails and staples.

Because of their shape, I have used the **corkscrew, can opener,** and **wire stripper** to help in bending the ends of metal, such as copper wire. They can also help with bent fishing hooks.

I'm going to be honest with you and say that there is one tool on the Swiss Army Knife that I have never used for its intended purpose: the **fish scaler.** But there are a few other things I have used it for. One of the things that used to annoy me after coming in from the field was having a bunch of burrs on my clothing. Sometimes they would hurt when picking them off, but mostly it just took forever to remove them, especially from my bootlaces! One day, I pulled out my Swiss Army Knife and noticed how the fish scaler was flat on one side, angled on the other, and didn't have any sharp edges. I ran the fish scaler along my clothing, and it knocked those burrs right off!

In the absence of a comb, I have used the teeth on the fish scaler to help separate hairs when looking for ticks, as well as to comb out my beard. When using it as a moustache comb, be careful not to accidently stick the hook disgorger in your nose.

You may find yourself with a model that has the **hoof cleaner tool** but no hoofed

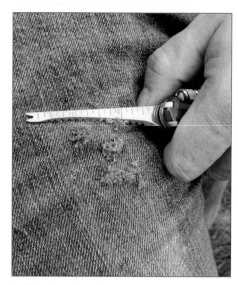

The fish scaler works great for this task, and since there aren't any sharp edges, I don't have to worry about hurting myself or damaging my clothing.

animals around. That's okay, because this beefy tool can be used in other ways. Use the frame of the Swiss Army Knife as a handle and the hoof cleaner to hook and grab onto items to make carrying them easier. It can be used to punch holes in materials. In extreme situations, it can be used as a small hammer to break open objects or for scraping purposes. (I know I stated earlier that the Swiss Army Knife should *not* be used as a hammer, which is why I said "in extreme situations.") It can be used to pull a stuck zipper on gear, to dig something out, and to pull on rope to avoid rope burns on your hands.

The Versatile Shackle Tool

At first glance, the shackle tool appears to only have a few functions, but that is just not true. The two obvious ways in which to use it are as a large sewing needle and for loosening the screw pin on a shackle. It actually has an array of uses, and to this day I am still finding more. Here's a quick top 10 ways you can use it—I'm sure you will find more!

1. Dislodge a hook that has found its way into your skin, by pulling on the body of the hook.

2. Use it like a small pick for digging and scraping purposes. The tip is much more robust than other tools on the Swiss Army Knife, so you don't have to worry about breaking it when digging in wood, fruits, nuts, or the ground.

3. Use it as a handy tracing tool when trying your hand at carving or engraving in wood.

4. Loosen small nuts and bolts by using it as a wrench.

5. Push cordage through small spaces with ease because of its thin profile.

6. Use it as a handle to lift items or to pull items by "hooking" onto them.

7. Use the two different-sized cutouts in the tool to tie off cordage when braiding, or to keep lines separated.

8. Use it like a pry bar and guide it in between two materials to separate them, since the tool doesn't have any sharp edges that could cut them. This is especially helpful when you need to separate bark from a log—a sometimes challenging task.

9. Push the straps on your pack through the buckles with this tool.

10. Use the openings in the tool to help bend pieces of metal, like fishhooks.

Here, I am using the shackle tool to loosen some knots in my shoes.

Be Prepared

Okay, so we cannot always be prepared for every situation all of the time. But there are some things to keep in mind when it comes to being better prepared for a bad situation. With the conveniences of everyday life and our advances in technology, we as people have become a bit lazy in our survival abilities. That is because we have become dependent on others for much in our lives and have all our needs readily provided. Turn on the faucet and clean water comes out. Head down to the store and you can pick and choose what you want to eat. The environments that we spend the majority of our time in are temperature-controlled without any effort on our part. We take all of this for granted and assume that it will always be like that. I don't view myself as having a doom-and-gloom personality, but I am also a realist and know that situations can change in an instant.

We may suddenly find ourselves in an extreme situation where having the ideal emergency supplies isn't possible. The truth of the matter is that most of us could easily be more prepared for everyday situations. My mantra has always been that knowledge and skills are more important than gear, because knowledge weighs nothing and cannot be lost. A good start is knowing basic first aid, how to find and purify water, using basic navigation in order to find a direction, knowing fire-starting methods,

---

A WORD OF ADVICE

Just because a tool breaks or becomes worn down, don't dismiss it as no longer being useful. For instance, when used heavily, the metal saw and file is a tool that will eventually become smooth and seemingly useless. This happened to one of my Swiss Army Knives in the past, and I had an idea on how to repurpose the saw. It took some work, and I did have the proper tools available, but I was able to turn the blank piece of metal into a knife. The next time this happens to one of my metal saws, I think I will attempt turning it into a shackle opener.

---

and how to stay cool or warm. When you have the knowledge, tools and supplies will naturally follow.

Prep Your Car

There is a lot of wasted space in a vehicle, and I urge people to use it. The vehicle is carrying the weight, so there is no burden on you. First, always have physical maps in your car. It doesn't take much for a phone to die or a signal to be unavailable. Knowing where you are and how to get where you want to go is critical. Have a first aid kit and a GHB (get home bag) in your vehicle every single day.

I live in an area that experiences both ends of the weather spectrum: extreme heat and cold. Never assume that everything is okay just because you are on a major roadway. It would not be unusual for me to have to spend hours, if not the night, in my vehicle due to bad weather. It doesn't matter how close you are to a town; if the weather is bad enough, first responders won't be able to get to you. Spending the night in your vehicle may not be life or death, but having some supplies will make the situation a lot more tolerable.

At a minimum, these are the items I like to keep in my vehicles at all times. It may seem like a lot, but it really doesn't take up that much space, and it can make a world of difference in a bad situation.

- Maps
- Swiss Army Knife
- A few bottles of water
- Food (granola bars, jerky, nuts, etc.)
- Blanket
- Extra set of clothes, including shoes or boots (this includes other weather-appropriate gear, coats, raincoat, umbrella, knit hat, gloves, etc.)
- Flashlight
- Lighter, matches
- Candles
- Something to write on and writing utensil
- Something for passing the time (such as a book or deck of cards)

Don't assume normal trips are always going to go to plan, because plans rarely hold up their end of the bargain. If you are going fishing, camping, hiking, biking, or even just going on a day trip somewhere, always plan ahead and take supplies that will help in case of a problem. It is always better to have something and not need it than to need it and not have it.

I endure a lot of teasing when going on small excursions like an overnight camping trip because of how I over prepare. For an overnight camping trip, most people would bring their coolers, maybe a change of clothes, and just enough food to last until they could get back to town. I always supplement this with cordage, tape, extra food, a water bottle, maps, clothes, fire-starting tools, and other supplies that would help in an emergency situation.

Let me present a scenario: Some friends go out on an overnight camping trip. Only enough food and drinks are brought to last the night, and they are 30 miles (48km) from the nearest town. They have a fun night sitting around the fire, eating good food, and telling stories. They wake up the next morning to find out that, for whatever reason, their vehicle won't start. They try to use their cells phones, but they can't get a signal, or they weren't able to charge their phones. Now someone, or everyone, has to walk to safety. Let's give this situation the benefit of the doubt and say they only have to walk 10 miles (16km) to a major roadway to flag someone down. That's not so bad! However, now a severe weather front moves in. Extreme heat, rainstorm, tornado, high winds, snow, etc. These conditions will not only limit their travel but limit the possibility of anyone else being out on the roadways. They may now have to spend another night or several nights out in the wilderness waiting for better travel conditions. Throw into the mix someone getting hurt or becoming sick and, well, you can see where I am going with this. This may sound a little far-fetched to you, but listen to the news. Situations very similar to this happen more often than you think.

According to a CBS report, in July 2018 a pair of hikers had to be rescued in New Hampshire's White Mountains by the Fish and Wildlife Department because the hikers were unprepared for the environment. (Read the full story at *https://minnesota.cbslocal. com/2018/07/07/hikers-rescued-minneapolis/.*)

In 2017, to celebrate the end of summer, a pair of teens hiked into the Grand Canyon. After becoming lost from the main trail, they had to spend several days rationing what little food they had before being rescued. (The story is online at *https://abcnews.go.com/US/teen-hikers-rescued-days-lost-grand-canyon-survived/ story?id=49413157.*)

These are two quick examples of the many situations like this that arise every year. So please be as prepared as you can before finding yourself in a wilderness situation. Remember, when we willingly venture into the wild unprepared, we are not only risking our lives but also those of the people who have to rescue us.

PART 4:

URBAN USES

This book explores how to use the Swiss Army Knife for outdoor survival situations. However, I wanted to share a few *non-survival* situations when the Swiss Army Knife saved the day for me. You just never know when one of these tools will come in handy.

Everyday Emergencies

Going Nowhere

I am not a fan of elevators. In fact, I do my best to avoid them. Due to the line of work I used to be in, I had to ride elevators frequently throughout the day. One day, I was riding the elevator by myself when suddenly it jerked to a stop. I pressed every floor button, but nothing happened. I pressed the alarm button, but there was no sound. I tried opening the emergency phone box, but its door was stuck. That's when the cab lights started flickering and I began to sweat. Short of pounding on the doors and yelling, it appeared that there was nothing I could do.

Then I remembered I had my Swiss Army Knife in my pocket. I quickly grabbed it and began using any and all of the tools to pry around the phone box door. After about ten minutes, I was able to pop it open and use the phone to call the front desk.

All Washed Up

Getting stuck in a public restroom is not fun, but it happened to me. After washing up, I reached for the doorknob and discovered that it didn't want to work. I knocked on the door loudly and called out, but nobody responded. It was time to take matters into my own hands once again.

I used the screwdriver on the Swiss Army Knife to remove the doorknob on my side, exposing the inner workings. From there I was able to slide the latch and free myself. Needless to say, the store clerk gave me a puzzled look when I handed him the doorknob and said that the bathroom was out of order.

Breaking In

I have even had to use the Swiss Army Knife to break into my own vehicle. It is not as dramatic as it sounds, but still interesting. After closing the door of my car, I realized that I had left the keys on the seat. Of course, the doors were locked. Luckily, I had left the windows open just a bit. They were not open enough for me to reach my arm in, but the opening was large enough for something else.

I broke off a nearby tree branch and, with the hook extended, I tied the Swiss Army Knife to the branch with my shoelace. The great fishing adventure began! It took me twenty-five minutes to hook onto the little bundle of keys, but I was able to retrieve them.

Pedal Power

There are many different modes of transportation, but in an emergency our options may become limited. Gas-powered vehicles may not be a viable way to travel. A bicycle may be your best bet, so you'll need to keep it in good shape. There are many things that a Swiss Army Knife can do if a bicycle needs repair.

Just like a car, bicycles can get a flat tire. The best option for fixing a flat is to replace the tire if you have access to a new one. Combining the can opener and bottle opener, you can create a leverage point between the spokes and the tire in order to remove the tire.

When we have to use a bike that is not ours, there are adjustments that may need to be made in order to make the ride more comfortable. The pliers on the SwissChamp make it much easier to raise or lower the seat, as well as the handlebars. Did the gear chain fall off or become stuck? Use the hook tool to help guide the chain to where it needs to be.

You should always be on the lookout for resources and never pass up an opportunity to obtain more. Some people might overlook an inoperable piece of equipment lying in a ditch, but very useful things can be scavenged from a bicycle. The tire spokes can be taken off to be used for fishing. Rubber from the tire can be burned to create black smoke for signaling purposes. The wire from the brake lines can be used as cordage.

Epilogue

What I have shown in this book doesn't even come close to the full potential of what the Swiss Army Knife can do. I don't think there would an end to a book like that. My goal for this book was to highlight the incredible versatility of the Swiss Army Knife. The little red knife is a powerhouse unto itself and can complete many of the same tasks that the "tactical," "trendy" knives can, and even more. The projects in this book are just the beginning, and I hope that you take the time to discover all you can do with your Swiss Army Knife.

Even in the darkest of situations, I have found that it is much easier to put one foot in front of the other if you can find the humor surrounding you. I didn't want this to be another emergency situation book that was all doom and gloom; there are enough of those in the world as it is. While emergency preparedness projects and learning how to be self-reliant can be serious material, they can also be fun if you allow them to be. To me, it isn't until we forget how to smile and laugh, especially at ourselves, that we are doomed.

Lastly, in this throwaway society that we live in, I wanted to stress the importance of properly cleaning and maintaining a tool like the Swiss Army Knife. From the first Swiss Army Knife that was made to the Swiss Army Knife that is rolling off the assembly line as you read these words, people have spent their lives ensuring that every knife is of the highest quality. By taking

Victorinox workers striving for perfection in their products in 1930, a year before automation was implemented.

care of something that is taking care of us, we are not only honoring those people's hard work and dedication, but placing value back into quality products.

Thinking back to the many conversations I have had about knives, I find it humorous how most people laugh at me for carrying a Swiss Army Knife. They are quick to pull out some version of the latest and greatest knife. Almost 100 percent of the time it is just a knife with no other tools, and that is all they are depending on. Don't get me wrong; a knife blade is an invaluable tool to have and I never go without one. But every morning when I get dressed, there is one knife that goes on my belt or in my pocket without fail, and it is usually my Victorinox SwissChamp.

A normal day can turn bad instantly, and if there was only one tool that I could have on my person when that happens, it would be my SwissChamp. I have that much faith in Swiss Army Knives. I have owned them. I have used them. I thoroughly enjoy carrying a Swiss Army Knife. I know that when you choose the right tool for the job and take care of it, a Swiss Army Knife can get the job done and be passed along to the next generation.

Bryan Lynch

Index

Index

Photo Credits

All artwork is by Nikki Lynch and the author except where noted below.

Courtesy of Victorinox: pages 6–8, 11, 12, 15, 17, 19, 21, 23, 25, 27, 29, 31–33, 35, 37–39, 42, 43 (left and center), 46, 222.

From Shutterstock.com: Catalin Petolea, page 109; Erik Klietsch, pages 5 (bottom left) & 62; frantic00, page 9; GaudiLab, pages 5 (bottom right) & 219; LMWH, pages 4 (bottom right) & 47; Marek Trawczynski, page 152; Nikifor Todorov, page 185; Photomario, back cover (background); PixMarket, page 73; PRESSLAB, page 176; Przemyslaw Wasilewski, page 1; REDAV, page 204 (right); rsooll, page 132; Sergii Sobolevskyi, page 150 (top); showcake, page 207; Tarik Kaan Muslu, front cover; twinlynx, page 113; Vlad Sokolovsky, page 169; Volodymyr Martyniuk, page 74; wow.subtropica, page 68.